The Calligraphy of God

JENIMDIBIE

THE CALLIGRAPHY OF GOD

For permission request, email us at:

Jenimcast@gmail.com

This is a work of fiction.

No character in this work is real or based on a real person, unless noted.

Printed in the United States of America.

Order this book online at www.amazon.com or at any other international Amazon website.

Book sales also available through other participating online stores and book stores.

This title is also available as an eBook.

ALSO BY JENIM DIBIE

Scarcast

I wrote this:

For the broken

For the whole

For the lost

For the found

For the wounded

For the healed

For the misfits

For the crowd

For the hidden

For the seekers

For the lonely

For the loved

For the hopeless

For the hopeful

For the world.

I wrote this for you.

Contents

My dream of being a published poet came true when Scarcast, my first book was published, and now I've been blessed with another opportunity to give you my heart in this book you are holding, The Calligraphy of God.

Poems have been my soul's way of healing its wounds and letting light flood through my broken parts. The blood that flows through my veins carries ink to my heart to help write the sadness back to happiness. This is a gift and I am not unmindful of that, so here I am giving you what I have been given.

I hope you enjoy reading The Calligraphy of God as much as I enjoyed writing it. I felt a tornado of emotions as I reread each poem.

As you read The Calligraphy of God, each page will leave you with a different emotion, and at your very last turn, I hope you'll smile and let out a sigh of hope.

Love,

Jenim.

Acknowledgments

A warm thank you to:

My parents — for their unrelenting love, prayers, and kindness.

Winifred Dibie — for showing me what love means.

Mildred Dibie — for her kind words and encouragement.

Tyrone Dibie — for always making me laugh out loud.

My friends and followers on Facebook, Twitter and Instagram — for keeping me on my toes and giving me a reason to never stop writing.

Everyone who made this book possible.

And finally a warm thank you to you holding this book.

May you find colour in my black.

Phoenix

I have always been a fire,

And everyone I loved,

Walked away as ashes,

Until I met a phoenix,

Who was born to love flames.

Longing

All the masks in my world
In search of one face
All the darkness in me
In search of one star
To make me breathe again
To make me see again.

Heart of Hearts

I'm in a frame of mind

You wouldn't want to frame in your mind

See, in my mind

I love you and show you so

But in your mind my love for you has withered
more

The space in time makes you no longer mine

This space in time takes my all, but that's fine

Though far from me and all these thorns

If you stay one more day, you'll see the roses born

Times like these have always been

The pain you bear I've always seen

On days like those that I don't seem to be your kin

Just know I bear my own sin

As the knives prod your delicate skin

May God be your life, your King

I will always love you but I am not God

I will sometimes hurt you because I am not God

But if someday, somehow, you see past the hurt

You will see a picture of you framed in the hall of
love

Known as my heart of hearts.

The Artist

When I see a broken person

I think of the God who made him

I'm perturbed by the artist who carved him

The moment transports me to a

World where love is

And I wonder why all I know is

How pain feels

I open my pocket and lock

All my troubles in it

And bring out the last

Shard of my heart

I offer him

And ask if

He'd like to know what God is.

Hell

Your eyes pull out light from my dark soul, and every moment with you transcends transcendental memories. Your love has been my heaven. Holding me closely in your arms, our heartbeats remind me that God exists. I wonder if you are human or an angel, and ask if this is what immortality feels like. You smile softly and then I see it. I see hell in your smile. A hell in which the sun sets never to rise again. You showed me your demons, I showed you mine. I wondered if we would ever heal or if time was just as broken too, and asked if this was what mortality felt like. You held my face in your hands and raised it long enough for me to see, a sun rising never to set again. You smiled gently and then I saw it. Hell was the absence of love and I was your heaven. And then you saw it... you were mine as well.

Threnody

One of my biggest battles, loneliest and longest journey in life has been arriving at a place where I make peace with myself. For the longest time, I was at war with my soul in my soul for my soul. I just unpacked my bags, and breathing freedom in for the first time, I exhale my story. I inherently lack the capacity to hate anyone, or to hold a grudge... I forgive as surely as I sin. A lot of people have hurt me and I have hurt a lot of people, the tragedy of both is that I blame myself for two. I forgive anyone for anything, except myself. When my mistakes hurt you, I loathe myself, when your mistakes hurt me, I despise myself. The burden has been heavy, and my walk, slow. Someone once described depression as rage turned inward, and I have been depressed for a very, very long time. You will never see my fists clench or my lips bleeding or my veins burst in anger, but you will see ink in my veins bleeding bruised words, and you will see "save me" hiding on my forehead. If you look closely, you would see a post office in my eyes filled with letters of apologies that have no forwarding addresses. You will see a sparrow in a corner waiting to soar, you will see no cage in there, but my own mind. The continuous feeling of being wrong made me keep apologizing for being right. I apologized for being me, till there was no one left to be sorry for. So I packed my bags, I cut the thread and left it all behind, in search of a person, place, or thing that thought that I was kind of beautiful. But no amount of peace outside could end the war inside. I kept looking outside me for the things inside me, till I was drained of every last drop of strength I needed to go on living. Like a kid in a sandbox, I played with tragedies of the past, not knowing how to forgive myself for the things I had done to myself, for the things I had done to others, for the things others had done to me. Then one day I looked at my hands, they were the hands of a ready writer, and I gazed at my soul, it was the soul of a poet, and I looked at my heart, it was broken enough to become words, and I stared at my spirit, it was starved enough to drink God. And when I looked past myself, there was a world beyond me. A world that needed me to love myself so much that I'd have enough love to give to those wandering the earth with "save me" written on their forehead. My gift has never been about me, it's always been about the ones I give it to. I can never truly say that I fully understand how I arrived here, but I've come to realize that, I am human, one worth forgiving, one worth loving with all of my broken heart.

Those Three Words

...And if I had no words,

I would still say I love you...

In more ways than three words.

The Note

The world is a dark place

Where I just dealt my last ace

So I exit to find the light

Maybe I will get lost in a maze

Maybe I will get God's praise

I hope that the other side is bright

I pray that eternity is void of night.

Remember To Stain the World

Remember to stain the world

With one last drop of your ink

With one last roar of your name

With one last brushstroke of your sins

With one last silence that begs forgiveness

With one last laughter that slays regret

With one last moment that paints a memory

With one last word that fills the distance between

"I" and "you"

Remember to stain the world

With every last drop of you.

Resurrection

Something died in me

And every word I've penned has been to resurrect it

My heart has become a rearview mirror

That looks always upon that moment in time

Where I was taken away from me

But how do I get to a future when my past is always present

How do I move on when my bones are made of lead?

I look up to the sky for beauty

The sky looks down at me for the same

So I empty my heart as poetry in a world filled with words

In hopes that one day when the sky looks at me

It would see a girl with full moons for eyes

A broken heart for stars

A lost soul for rain

A body of clouds

Unrelenting hope for rainbows

And the passion of a hundred million suns.

The Sea

Sometimes I long to belong to the sea, to be a vast, meaningful nothingness... that's loved by a shore. I run away most times from no one but me, to be with the breeze, to be alone with the storm inside me. My smile has become a mask for a pain that has no face.

Sometimes I long to belong to someone, to linger in their every thought, to be their first thought before coffee and their last before blankets. To be their dream come true.

I'm a dreamer who's found the kindest realities in dreams. My imagination has been heaven for my wandering soul. 'Cause there I belong to me, and I'm at peace with me, and no labels are glued on me, and my face breathes free.

But I wake up every morning drowning in oxygen, and my voice travels for miles and miles as written words in a bottle, swimming to the feet of someone who longs to be the sea, to be a vast, meaningful nothingness that's loved by anyone.

Punctuation Marks

You sit alone with the

Lonely crowd inside you

All they have to say are

Words that slit your soul

To bleed in eternal silence

You remember the happiness

You once found in a moment

You somehow lost to memories

All that is left in your hands

Is a sadness that's

Drawn four lines across each palm

It's the only map you have

And all its roads lead to nowhere

You close your eyes and

All you see is darkness

Yet your mind sees a light so bright

It blinds all your fears

But your broken wings

Cannot carry you high enough

To be touched by it

Your ribs are cracking

And your heart is falling out

Everything beats faster in one final

Full stop

The Poet and the Pain

If I was a poet

I would have

Found the

Right words

By now

And the need to

Keep write, write, write, writing

Would have faded

Away with the pain

But the silence overwhelms me

So I break it with words

And call it poetry

But what if

Silence was all the poetry I needed?

What If

Some days I am afraid to write

So I choke on

The words that can only be written

I start with a word

And end with that word

Afraid that the whole might break the parts

What if we learned to write our hearts?

What if our broken hearts become beautiful works
of art?

Buried deep beneath your fears

Are your dreams

Live them.

In Dreams

As the night draws

The curtain upon our lives

The stage is set

For our dreams to come alive

In dreams we love and live

In dreams we dance and sing

In life we dream of love

In life we leave our dreams

In life we live our dreams.

Moth

I loved you

With the heat

Of a million suns,

For I knew

No other

Way.

The Rose

I think of you ever so often

I think of you as a flower

A flower arched to a rising sun

I remember when I first saw you

You blossomed as I held your hand

Many seconds have evaporated since that moment

And the rain that made you grow

Was the rain that crushed you when you had
blossomed

And though your flower withered

Your fragrance is forever captured in my soul.

I Miss You

My heart is tired and my eyes are heavy, but sleep won't come to these aching bones. You are in my thoughts and you are in my memory, and in every part of me you never even touched. It makes me wonder, if you held my hand, or if you waved your hand or if a kiss goodbye would have been enough to make me not miss you.

Oxygen

The air that keeps me alive

Has little to do with oxygen

It has everything to do with

Your kiss that breaks and fixes me

All in one moment

And the seeds you sowed

In the broken parts of me

And the wars in my mind

You fought with me

And your strength

That lets my weakness

Fall to the ground

The air that keeps me alive

Has nothing to do with oxygen

It is the love you taught my soul to inhale

And my heart to exhale.

This Gift You Have Given Me

The more tightly I held on to you

The more freely you slipped away

It took my heart a lifetime

To understand that

Nothing is ever mine

Everything is given

And all things will be taken away.

The Writer

Sitting by the telephone

Waiting for my life to call me

I heard time say

Each day is a blank page

Write on it what you will.

No Regrets

Dragging my shadow down the street

The sun shines light on my regrets

The things I should have done

But left undone

The things I shouldn't have done

But did

Goodbye where I said hello

Hello where I said goodbye

Words where silence should breathe

Silence where words should scream

Trying to take back all

The words I never said

Dying to give you all

The words I cannot say

Ashes fill up a yellow sun

As the night begins to rise

I sit alone, my soul and me

Waiting on the rain to wash away

My wild, wild sea.

What Makes You Strong

There is a world inside me

That is painted with colours that do not exist

There is a word inside me

That cannot be written or read

Every life is like a book

There is always a chapter

That would bring you to tears

My life has been a hundred of those pages

And my days are spent hitting rocks at the bottom
of an ocean

But some days I come up for air

And I feel life gracing my lungs

It feels so good to be alive those days

And I see clearly how

Everything that drowned me

Taught me how to swim.

Man on the Moon

Show me what songs would make you fly

And I will play them for you

Upon broken heartstrings

Tell me what words would make you smile

And I will write them with blood on paper

Show me what love would let you breathe

And I will breathlessly let you go, to it

But love takes breath

Before it gives it

Bright skies become dark clouds

Before they weep rain

Seeds die in darkness

Before trees dance in the light

And you, my darling, know that

It's always darkest before the morn

Your songs of sorrow will bring you joy

The breath you hold will soon be exhaled

The tears that fall will water your seed

And you will find me there in the corner

Writing you a poem, with my whole heart

Singing you a song, with my whole soul

Breathtakingly letting you breathe

With my whole spirit

As you begin to dance, in your rain

As you begin to fly, to your light

As you begin to be, your own sun.

Blessed

I never found the tomorrow

You promised would be alright

But I learned that being alive

Was a blessing in its own right

So I thanked you for today

And felt a little bit alright.

Of Poets and Skies

We write in silence about sound

We write in sadness about happiness

We write in tears about laughter

We write alone about a crowd

We write of light from utter darkness

We paint stars from a dark room

We offer insight from our confusion

We write of freedom from a cage

We pen the sky from beneath a sea

We write of love with ripped out hearts

We pen beauty from our pain

Our heart is our pen

And our blood is our ink

Our scars are our words

And our hope hides in-between our lines

We write of home from abandoned buildings

We go to bed alone at night

Writing love poems on the cold side of the pillow

Closing our eyes hoping to see

A world where we are free indeed.

The Light

The end of the tunnel

Has been hard to think of

From this depth of darkness

I have been hidden in

Nothing makes sense anymore

Not even what my heart whispers

I have tried to reach for light

But the light seems to be made for

Everyone but me

Some have lovers

Some have dreams

I have an abyss that wouldn't

Let me go.

Forgive & Forget

I hope my forgiveness reminds you,

Of the part you forgot to break in me.

Stay

Only say goodbye

When the rain falls upward

When the sun shines at midnight

When the world becomes flat

When dogs begin to speak

When forever is now

When love is not a drug

When life is void of pain

When everything becomes nothing

Only say goodbye when...

Time returns me to dust

Where goodbye is not a word.

Hello, Goodbye.

You said hello

Then

All was quiet but the

Beating of our hearts.

You said goodbye

And

All fell silent but the

Breaking of my heart.

Happy Endings

Read me until my words make you hold me

Kiss me until the air in my lungs is emptied in yours

Hold me until all of me becomes a part of you

Love me until fate begins to write happy endings.

My Art

I wish I could leave me sometimes,
That I could walk away,
Far enough to stare at me,
To peer through my windows,
Into my vagabond soul.
My brown eyes seem to ask me:
What have I become?
Am I still beautiful,
Or just plain broken?
Can I still love with these sharp fragments?
That which didn't kill me,
Left me bleeding,
Left me fearful,
Left me doubtful,
Of the faith I see trembling
In my clenched fists,
Of the dreams I see slipping
Through my wet eyes,
Of the hope that's still swimming
In my Atlantic heart.
I wish I could hold me sometimes,
Tight enough to rearrange these turbulent pieces
Into a mosaic of peace.

Renaissance

I cling to the thought of you like the air I breathe. So invisible, yet so powerful. I couldn't live without you and I haven't lived without you in more ways than one. I could never hold air, and I had to let go of your slippery hand, but like the oxygen in my lungs, you remain in my heart. Like the haem in my heart, you gave me life. You remained in my mind, like a human photograph, standing in front of me. Silently tearing me apart, so unshakeable, utterly unforgettable. Like the carbon dioxide gushing out my nostrils, the time has come for me to let every breath of you I took in, out. For me to let me grow and blossom into a flower that loves another just as deeply as I loved you. I will miss you like dead things miss oxygen. I will rise up like dead seeds become great trees. I have written you in every poem, you are forever smeared on the pages of me. Your touch is still tattooed on my skin but today I bathe in the light of day, and as the rays tangle up around my face and body, the darkness of your absence would be washed away from my soul. And as the clouds gather up above my head, in one, two, three moments... I will be born again.

Tattoo

On my skin is written

All the things

My soul

Cannot scream.

In The End

When I think of you now
I remember the beginning
I always think of you
So I'm always stuck at the start
When love was a promise
A thousand and one butterflies
Fluttering relentlessly in my gut
I try to forget the end
When love was a sad song tearing through my
cracking heart
I can't remember what you looked like in those
moments
When you waved goodbye, and your hand covered
your face
And my tears blinded my eyes
And a silence engulfed the distance between A and
where you'd B
I can't see you through clouded skies
I wait for your star on these darkest of nights
But in me are cities built on the graves of dead
butterflies
And every day feels like a funeral
For the things that cannot be.

Homeless

When people leave and

The home you built for them

Remains

Dust begin to gather

Cobwebs string the rooms

Silence empties where their laughter once filled

And when you think to fix the broken doors

A knife cuts through your heart

And you shut the doors forever.

The End

We run from our shadows

In hopes of finding ourselves

But ourselves hold shadows too

Like light carries darkness

And when we get to our destination

We will find that

All we ran

Away from

We ran

Into.

Shock Value

When a storm hits

And the storm fades

And you are still standing

Yet, still afraid

Of the worst

That has come

And gone

You spend the rest of your life

Standing still.

Room for Two

Life is a series of rooms.

In that room I loved you

The best I could

In the way I knew

In this room I'm standing alone

Held by the cold winter wind

I've felt pleasure

I've known pain

I've danced my heart out

I've cried my eyes out

I've jumped for joy

I've bled my soul

I've fallen to rise again

I've risen to fall again

I've felt summer

I've known winter

I've been autumn

I've loved spring

I'm the sum of the parts

I'm the good and the bad

As the door opens

On the next room

May I find me.

Haunted

My heart is now an empty house

A love that once visited it

Haunts it

Our first kiss reenacts on the corridors

And the answering machine replays

Our countless "I love you"

And the warmth of your body chills the walls

As footsteps creep toward me

I crawl to the corner of my own heart

And wrap myself in my own arms.

Gravity

Lying on green grass

Beneath a blue sky

I watched as my fear of falling

Buried my dream of flying.

The One

My heart's been broken in a thousand pieces,

I've lived and died a thousand times,

And in each of those lifetimes,

With all of those pieces,

I chose you...

A million times.

Consectatio Felicitatis

I said:

I am a poem in search of her poet

A painting longing for its artist

A world looking for her creator

I am a vast empty page

Aching for one drop of ink

He said:

I am your poet

And you will love me for my words.

Tango

I am the poet

You are the poem

I hold the pen

You are the words

Love is the ink

Silence is the blank page.

Family Portrait

A room hung with pictures

A room stained with memories

A tear hiding in your iris

A smile frozen for the camera

The cheese before the shutter

The happy family asks for

A portrait framed with secrets.

The Mask

Sadness has always worn the

Most beautiful masks and

The widest smiles often

Conceal a gaping wound

Hidden in winter is

The promise of spring even

A well of sorrow can

Fetch a bucketful of

Laughter, even

Stars shine only in

Darkness, even

The sun still exists at night

All hope is

Never lost

Only frozen in

Frost.

Hush

I clothe my words when mad

I say no words when scared

I cut my words to fit you

I find my thoughts in rock songs

I swallow your words, the swords

I drown my words in thoughts

Until my thoughts died as words

Now I'm trying to take back

All the words I never said.

Happily Never After

I was a rainbow

I fell in love with

A boy like rain

One of us faded away

One of us remained.

Chamber of Secrets

There is a story in my chest

That has so much to say

Except when I try to say it

The chambers of my heart

Let out a long sigh

Which is to say

There's nothing left

To say.

Everything Ends

There are paths I never dreamed of taking, that I've taken. There are things I never imagined doing, which I've done. The universe has a funny way of introducing you to yourself anytime you say "never". Except it's not that funny, and you may not want to meet yourself. The road is hard and treacherous, the nights are dark and lonely, with no moon to hold you, with no stars to guide you. You'll lose your compass along the way, you'll try to drown at sea, you will stand still and try to crumble to dust. Everything good will not come easy, anything easy would not be that good. You'll reach for everything and grasp nothing, you'll pray for anyone and find no one, you'll pray to anyone to be someone for you.

The only reprieve you'll find is underwater, but you know if you stay down long enough, you'll run out of air, you'll run out of... will. So you come up for air and breathe in nothingness, and find solace in the company of your own arms.

There are days when it seems that nothing you do is alright, that nothing you are is good enough. But the nature of life begins with one truth: Everything ends. Even the broken thoughts searing your mind. Even the darkest dark gives way to light. Even the pain no words can describe. The hourglass has a way of turning, and life becomes a mixture of contradictions - the hope and the despair, deep sorrow and ecstatic joy, the passion and the pain, the silence screaming, the screams silent, the longing and the filling, the losing to find again, the utter darkness and the blinding lights, the dreamed life, the dying to live another day, the living to fight another day.

There is a me I never thought I could become, there are wounds I never knew could heal. But here's to a journey full of life, and to destinations no one thought we could ever reach. Cheers.

The Innocence of Innocence

I want to see the world through your eyes

To look through that brown glass

And see beauty in the darkest dark

To catch a glimpse of hope

Holding the trembling hands of my despair

To watch love clean wounds that life inflicted

To observe the moon dying at dawn

That the sun may live

To stare at the sun as it dies at dusk

Just so the moon can breathe again

To believe in a God I cannot see

And have faith in things that cannot be

To take off my masks finally knowing

That it's perfectly okay to be a flawed human being

If only my eyes could see with all your heart

I'll know that where I break is not where I end

And when I fall is not when I die

But where I rise

Above it all

The pain and the loneliness

The hurt and its blindness

My mistakes and their judgment

Where I fall is where I rise

To fight another war

To live another day

To love even harder... in a better way

Till the night I fall again and can rise no more

To see the world through innocent eyes.

Strength

Which has broken me more

Love or hope?

The more I'm broken

The more I exhale beauty

My heart walks on water

Even after it's been drowned

My soul aches for sunlight

Even though it's become night

This is how it was created to love

This is how I go on living.

The Calm Is the Storm

Love, a home that is at once

A storm and a shelter

Love, breaks your heart

Into more pieces than

It is made of

Love, fixes you and ships you

Back to the battlefield

Love, a sea I want to swim in

Love, an ocean that drowns me

Love, takes my breath away

Love, makes me write air

Love, the words and the silence

Love, the silence in between the words

Love, the comma and the exclamation point

Love, full stop.

YOU

I hope you know that even though

I walk away from you

More often than the

Sea abandons the shore

I love you

I hope you know that even though

All my world is a stage

I would love to slow dance with you on it

I love you

I hope you know you are the words

To my favourite poem

The lyrics to my favourite song

My favourite book in the world's library

I love you.

Good Night

Oh sleep

Kiss my eyes

And take me

To other worlds

Where the monsters are

In my head and not my bed

And love is

In my bed and not my head.

Somewhere In The Middle Of Nowhere

I know where nowhere is
I know where nowhere leads
It's the place you go when you have
Nothing left to lose but you
It's a place that lunges at the emptiness in sight
It's a place where you scream when you're mad
It's a place where you weep when you're sad
It's a place where you scream and light up the sky
It's a place where you come to kneel and say a word
that's called a prayer
It's a place where no one is... but you
It's a home no one visits... but me
To look for someone who was drowned
In the droning noise of the somewhere
Where everyone everywhere in the world
Wanted to be and be seen
Where everyone wants to be
Where everyone begs to be seen
Where everyone comes to be someone
Who more often than not is no one similar
To who they really are when you
Close the door and turn off the light
It's a place where love is who you are
Not a rush of feelings that punches your gut

A place where no creed or race or division
Has ever found its way across the borders
A place where the religion is love and the race is
human
And the language is love written in Braille
A place where the fall of one is the fall of all
And the rise of one is the job of all
I learned that light shines brighter when you can
taste the darkness
That light finds its meaning in the darkest dark
I know a place called Nowhere right there
In the middle of nowhere
Where your soul rests and you face breathes
Away from the masks, away from the façade of the
crowd
Away from the glory of somewhere to
The earthy charm of nowhere
Where your soul finds you and shows you just
where
To go to remain true to you.

Strangers

Love is a wanderer who builds homes in people

You would walk past Love

If you saw her

She looks nothing like

Your poems

She's just a stranger

With an ocean in her eyes

And a worn-out story.

Love Story

Love is the thorn you bear

To make her a rose

Love is what the sea does to the shore

Love is how the shore waits for the sea

Everyone is a love story

Written in Braille

If you close your eyes long enough

You can read them page by page

You will see them through and through

Our love is a portrait of the sea and shore

Intermittent

But

Always.

Sands

The sea says I love you

To the shore

Without a word muttered

Just a silent promise

Engraved by an endless touch

Your skin will forever be my home.

 Lost

When you feel it hurting

But cannot say how it feels

You lose yourself

Reading a stranger's words and finding yourself in them

Like looking into another's eyes and finding your soul in them

I have nothing more to heal you with

Than these words that I've been given

So as ever as your heart remains night

May these words be stars for you.

I'm Sorry

Transiting through time

                      Like an apology

                                    In

Search

          Of its mistake.

Full Moon

Weakness and strength are

Two halves of the same moon

Like darkness and light

Like fear and faith

Like despair and hope

Like hate and love

Like my head and my heart

Like fiction and truth

Like misery and joy

Like a rose and its thorns

Like you and me.

Silent Word

Words are life

Words are living

Words are swords

Words can break you

Faster than they

Can mend you

Words can show you

What's screaming in

The silence

If you dwell in

Silence long enough

You will become

Words.

Celestial

Staring across a crowded room

Your soul looked like it would never be lost again

Your eyes locked mine in the hole of a minute

And filled my veins with enough blood to love your
heart for a lifetime

I knew the hourglass would spin too fast for me to
catch your falling sands

And learned a treasure that beautiful belonged to
someone else

I remember all the moments when you saved your
secrets inside my vault

I forget all the memories that wish I could hold you
again, for a moment

On my darkest nights you sat as a star beside me

You became a mirror that reminded me I was a
treasure too

I loved you in the silence between heartbeats

From that moment till my last breath.

The Sky

I once met a boy with two full moons for eyes

That made the stars in my night twinkle for a while

His words were raindrops and his heart was the sun

His laughter was thunder

And his sorrows cast a shadow

I once met a boy with heaven for a soul

My heartbeats became aves

And each bird loved the clouds

Whether it had rainbows, whether it rained

I once met a boy with a dream in his dreams

I wondered what made him forget to fly

His broken wings or his broken heartstrings

So I wrote him a poem called The Sky

To remind him why he could fly.

Promised Land

I promise you a land of fire
Where the winter of your life remembers spring
And all your flowers rise to my morning sun
I promise you a land of me
Where the hills and valleys are the curves of my
body
And every touch is a poem with a thousand words
written in silence
I promise you a land of water
Where every sin is washed away in a sea of
forgiveness
And every tear would fall on the desert of my chest
Where your lonely soul would swim in the deep
seas
Of my eyes
And all your demons would be devoured by the
storm
I promise you a land called love
Where my every heartbeat is a song called you
And every kiss is a poem of innocence
And every fight is a glue that fixes us
And every moment is a portrait of forever
A land where all I am is a space that graces you
With the time of your life.

Home

If I had a world of my own,
Everything would be my own,
Everywhere will be my home,
No one would be alone.

God has a world all his own,
And everywhere is his home,
Yet he leaves everyone on their own,
To roam till they find their home.

Everything is as it seems,
Nothing is as it is,
The less you see, the more you look,
The more you see, the less you dream.

Who is it I wanted to be sober,
I forgot her as I grew older,
But remember I am much sadder,
Than I ever was as a toddler.

I was much *muchier* than I am now,
Oh, everything fades don't ask me how,
Just set your hands to the sky,
And wave the birds you love goodbye.

So, you have everything you want and can say,
All the world's your stage for certain,
Yet time is just an aching play,
That closes everyone's curtain.

If I had a world of my own,
I would want you to be my home,
I would be the cage you run from when you are
mad,
I would be the sky you fly to when you are sad,

If I could have a world of my own,
I wouldn't have a world of my own,
I would just be your own,
You would just be my home.

Shipwrecked

All my goodbyes didn't know how to leave you behind

All my apologies didn't know how to rap on the door of their mistakes

All I wanted was for my life to have a good beat I could drum to

All I needed was to find you lost without me

All silence is a sad song looking for its lyrics

All our moments broke into memories

All our wishes became horses

All we are misses who we were

All I am is a space in time

All in time will be just fine.

Faith

Looking through windows

For the ones who'll come

For the one who'd stay

Asking dumb questions

To break an intelligent silence

To fill the awkward air

To ask if I'm here

To know if anyone knows where here is

No tree pens poems on paper

They just speak to the winds in poetry

Sometimes I wonder if I speak in dead languages

And if the living will ever not misunderstand me

A soul is the distance between two wings

I was born with a wing by my side

And all my flights have led me to the ground

Love has been a journey to find one more wing

Life is the wind that sometimes lets me see the sky

And other times reminds me that I am gravity

I look out windows to look for a moment

Where my eyes will meet yours and set our souls on fire

But my pocket is full of memories made of stones

And I sink to the floor of an ocean that once loved me

I'm forever in the embrace of never

And time is a song that ends with my breath

I look outside to see what lies ahead of me

I get this feeling that my future is somehow behind me

I look for you in the ripening grains

In the setting sun, in the pouring rain

I look for you in every unanswered prayer

And die each day to see you live

I know the world calls this madness

I think God calls it faith

I feel the breeze walking away

As the window closes.

Behind A Dark Cloud

Daddy saw me today

He saw through the darkness that

Blinded the light that once was me

He saw a rainbow weeping

Behind the darkening cloud that now was me

He said he loved me

I hated me for making him love me

I couldn't let anyone love anything but

The door shutting behind the girl

That now was me.

Dance With Me

I will write you words

I will sing you songs

And slow dance to your heartbeats

But my heart is a poem

That aches to be read

By your heart.

Crying

It is one of the most beautiful things

An aching, sad feeling

That helps broken people go on living

It is how I talk to God

How I ask him what this life is about

It is how I release the pain I feel from the ever poking rod

How I let it all out

Sometimes I think the sky understands how I feel

I mean what else could rain mean

It's only natural to let your eyes peel

Taking all the sky has seen

But tears aren't the only symbol of crying

In fact, most art are some form of dying

That helps the artist go on living

I remember the first time I really cried

The tightness in my chest

I thought I had died

But it was just the beginning of the best

Days of my life

I may never understand the depths of the ocean
inside me

But tonight he asked me to be his wife

You should have been there to watch the floor
become a sea

Yea, joy can hit your gut so hard

Your eyes begin to see the stars that twinkle in the
darkest dark

And though life is a bittersweet party that drives me
mad

Hope makes me think that one day I'll turn around
and see God having my back

Then I'll cry on his shoulder

And feel all better.

It Is How We Grow

It is in the nature of man to war

To fight, to sound the battle cry at the threat to his existence

It is in the nature of life to test mankind

To pull him by the short hairs and make him say "please"

To show him a volcano, and throw him into it

To make him play by the waterside

And dip his head in what seems like a pond but really is an ocean

It is in the nature of man to fight nature

To see everything he is, hate everything he is, and recreate all he is

And name the new man, Mr. Better Man

It is in the nature of man to fight his foes, which more often than not, are his friends

It is in the nature of man to fly, a nature unseen by all blinded by the great fall

But those who remember to look will see, they will remember the sky - they will remember home

It is in the nature of man to eat adversity all the days of his moonlit life - it is his daily bread

But on the day that man would raise his hands to the clouds

And shift the moon to pick a star and find that star bears his name

It will be a great day if he pulls down the dark clouds, to see a higher light - the sun

It is in the nature of man to eat the dust, to accept defeat,

To confess the bleak, to cry over the milk

That is laying on the floor waiting for man to clean it up

It is in the nature of man to pass the salt, to pass the blame

It is in the nature of the sky to brew a storm, and the sea to clap for it,

The sky and the sea and all we see conspire to break any man found whole still

To the man whose whole life experiences can be summed as "hard"

The sky to him is made of brass, and the earth of iron

He understands not the world he was thrust into, nor the world him

The days are but a cold war, with no love to thaw the chill

In the depths of days which shine as night, it is in the nature of man to fold

In the emptiness of a naked soul, I found a seed which thrives

It is in the nature of man to wage wars against the enemies without

And die silently at the hands of the enemy within - himself

The devil in him, smiles with him, eats with him, and is him

The greatest battle he'll ever fight is the battle called him

It is in the nature of man to be blind, to think he sees, yet truly is blind to all he sees

He is blind to the world in him, yea, inside of him

The will, the power, the love, the strength, the light, the fight, the sight, the him in him

And this blind man expends his life fighting the world that is waiting for him to find himself

Yea, I know a seed which grows in the cruelest winter

In the deepest sea that drowns your soul

A seed that thanks the darkness for its "darken-ness"

A seed that grows through growing pains

A seed that waits for the rain to fall through the windows of man's own soul

The seed falls to the ground and silently, it dies

And starts to grow at the first drop of rain

It is the aching metamorphosis of a man that finds the man

It is in the nature of man to be carried by the days to his grave

Without knowing what really it is this all means

We often get lost in this chaotic maze we call the world

Every day we sell our souls in exchange for something

And when the lights go out and the men go home

We cover our heads beneath a pillow and soak our beds with what's left of our soul

The pain of a poet frightens all, but the music born from the pain is oft named a Poem

The insanity of an artist makes him miserable, but the child of his misery is called a Masterpiece

The uncertainty of a scientist keeps him awake at night, his insomnia, the world knows as Genius

The breaking of the human heart is painful, but what could love more than a broken heart?

The insanity of the human mind is a solitary affair, but what could create more than a broken mind?

The hollowness of the human spirit is a deadly thing, but what seeks God more than a broken spirit?

Brokenness is the mother of that seed

It creates a hole that lets the light in to synthesize a man

Into a stronger man

A kinder man

A lighter man

A hopeful man

This is how we know

This is how we grow.

Little Things I Know

There are things that are not to be said

Things that are not to be known

That lies beneath wandering souls

That hides within white picket-fenced homes

There are letters the moon will write to the sun

Sonnets the shore will write to the sea

Poems the desert will pen to the rain

Whispers a bird will sing to its cage

Lyrics wounds will rhyme to time

That may never be heard, that may never be read

There are things that live unknown

A quiet kind of innocence lives in not knowing

There are songs that die unsung

Truths that fade unspoken

Wines that flow untasted

To all the things we do see, we have a blind spot

And we do not see what we cannot see

And do not clearly see what we do see

We only see things as we are

All that lies beneath our clay

Is all we really are

Yet it takes faith to believe that I am a spirit with a soul

What's more real than the light you see

It's the darkness you can taste and touch

What's more real than the soul I'm told I am

It's the hole in me, the size of Texas

The echo is often the answer to my question

The body is the house of the soul

Yet the soul leaves the body in search of a home

I have always found home to be a person

I want to go home but I don't know who that is

The human soul is carved to wander

The human mind is crafted to wonder

The human body was chiseled to surrender

All that I am is all I do not know that I am

Once you get to know me...

Would you please help me get to know me

There are wounds that time cannot scar

There are words that sorry cannot bury

There are truths that lies cannot cover

There are songs a cage cannot cage

There are rains the heavens cannot hold

There are days the sun will need to cry

There are nights the moon will let out sigh

There are nights the stars will not come out and shine

There are stories hidden in the whispers of the wind

There are apologies that die in search of their mistakes

There are loves to give and no one to take

There are open eyes that are blinded from seeing

There are words that have no silence

There are silences that are lost for words

Seeking freedom, we move from one cage into another

Too often we write to our cage: You are my freedom

Oh, we write of freedom from a cage

The human spirit is the freest bird I know

The human mind is the only cage I know

The human body is the biggest wound I know

The human soul is the only wanderer I know

As I wander in the wonders of words formed from A-Z

I'm reminded that all that I know is I really don't know what I think I know.

All I Am

Looking into the eyes of the sea,

I see everything going up and falling down,

Like tides that hide as waves,

Slapping the shores ceaselessly,

As if trying to write its secrets on sands,

And cannot help but come back to wash them off...
again,

I see people opening veins, as if trying to bleed out
a memory,

And they dress up, as if threads can stitch a
wounded soul,

Your long goodbyes cut the thread that stitched
you,

And your long hugs leave the needles inside me,

Time is an ache that demands to be felt,

And you feel it as your hands graze a wrinkle on
your face,

All the time you spent asking what life meant,

Life spent collecting what your time meant,

Life is a dream you live by waking,

And the deepest holes in the world are found in people,

Oh, I wish that I could fill your emptiness,

But all I am is a space in time,

I see your skin stained by letters and apologies,

And I wonder what it is that makes your soul bleed,

I see all the self-destruct buttons you hide as the rain washes your skin,

And I wonder how I can make my umbrella cover your fractured soul,

I wish that you would know that,

The wind that blows out all your candles will one day make you a wildfire,

And that if the wind doesn't carry you to shelter,

It may be because it knows that the storm is your glory, and the sea, your home,

But if your eyes must rain, let it pour upon my desert,

I promise you a land of me, with a roof made of warm arms,

With kisses as deep as the sky weeps,

And sands made for just your hourglass,

Now, promises like people are made to be broken,

And sometimes even a sea drowns of thirst,

But my promises are me, and when I'm broken you
will be found in me,

On the days I couldn't breathe, I learned to paint
air,

So that on the nights that you cannot breathe, I will
become oxygen for you,

I have learned that everything ends,

So I welcomed the breaking of my heart,

And hid the fragments in-between the sands of
your hourglass,

Now, the broken and the beautiful have something
in common,

And the lucky and the loved are often the same
people,

This poem was meant to be a short song,

Of stolen kisses and missing heartbeats,

But my heart went on and on and on about I and
love and you,

In truth, all I wanted to say was,

I love you, and that is all there is to me.

Storm

My head knows the true story

My heart knows the love story

My body is torn into a story that aches

For nothing more than to be loved, truly

But life is a love story

And in the end, all the characters die

But before they do, they get a chance to love

And by loving they truly live

Love is a life story

Of hopes dashed against rocks

Of dreams buried by fears

Of winds helping wings fly

Of gravity pulling eagles down

How many times have your memories

Kept you from enjoying the moment

How many times have your true colours faded

Just because the world was colourblind

What colour of clothing do your fears wear

To the funeral of your dreams

Every dream is a lifetime hidden in a life

Beautiful storms dress in women's clothing

Can't live with them, can't live without them

The storm is a girl like me, who loves to destroy,
and destroys

I am a girl like the storm, who wants to love, but
destroys

Life is a journey that ends with you realizing

That the destination was the journey all along

Love is a map that leads you to itself

I have always been a fire

And everyone I ever touched became ashes

And when I walk away, they rise

And shine sitting next to another star

Now, I write to create a sky where

The moon can touch the sun and not get burned

And I write to forget the days that

Broke me into a million nights

But the darkness of my nights made

Me fall in love with stars

And my day began like all days begin - as a dark night

Every night will one day break into shards of sunlight

Every day will someday rest in the darkness

Oh, how quickly the days become yesterdays

How silently our summers fade to rain

A storm is a calm that tapped his feet

Everything that broke you made you great

Love is how life dances to the tap of the storm.

Old With You

Would you

Still read

Me

When

I

Become

A blank page?

Cornerstone

In a forest of doubt

I found faith

In a fallen leaf.

Not Afraid

What would you do if you were unafraid

Would you paint the world with hues of you

Would you whisper your name to the raging winds

And let the world know your story

What would you do if you were unafraid

Would you write a poem and then some more

Would you paint your soul and then the world

Would you love with all your heart

Would you give out that last piece of that broken heart

Would you say "I love you" one more time

What would you do if you were unafraid

Would you say how you feel

Would you still have a heart of steel

Would you close your eyes to see

What would you do if you were unafraid

Would you sit in a quiet room

Would you open all the letters that silence wrote you

Would you listen to the three tired hands of an old clock

What would you do if you were unafraid

Would you let down your hair

Would you not paint your face

Would you throw away all your masks

What would you do if you were unafraid

Would you sit behind that desk

Would you chase your dreams

Would you live in the wild

Would you love wildly

Would you spend your life with the birds

Or would you spend it wishing you had wings

What would you do if you were unafraid

Would you spend your life being afraid

Would you abandon the fragile hands of fear

Would you go on a walk with who you are

What would you do if you were unafraid

Would money be the god that guards your heart

Would you love the things you hate

Would you hate the things you love

What would you do if you were unafraid

Would you stand in front of the crowd

Would you be lost in the crowd

Would you be the crowd

What would you do if you were unafraid

Would you be the answer to someone's prayer

Would you drink the pain away

Would you paint the pain away

Would you pray the pain away

What would you do if you were unafraid

Would you dance in a room full of no one

Would you fly

Would you dance with me

What would you do if you were unafraid

Would you love everyone

Would you love anyone

Would you love you

What would you do if you were unafraid

Would you be afraid of being unafraid

Would you be unafraid of being afraid

What would you do if you were unafraid?

Gone

What if I said it

Gets harder at night

The thoughts get louder

The stars don't shine here

And I am lost for words

In this moment

Held by your absence

Everything makes me cry

Even the memory of your presence.

Rain

All was quiet today

But the registering of time

By the old grandfather clock

Hanging on the beige wall

I looked around my heart

And there was no one in there

There was no one I wanted to call

There was no one who wanted to call me

There was no one I wanted to hold

There was no one who wanted to hold me

Me

A vessel holding a

Rainbow painted with colours that do not exist

Me

A storm that wants to love

But destroys everything in its path

Me

The answer to nobody's question

All was silent today but

The dark clouds gathering in my heart

That rained through

My eyes.

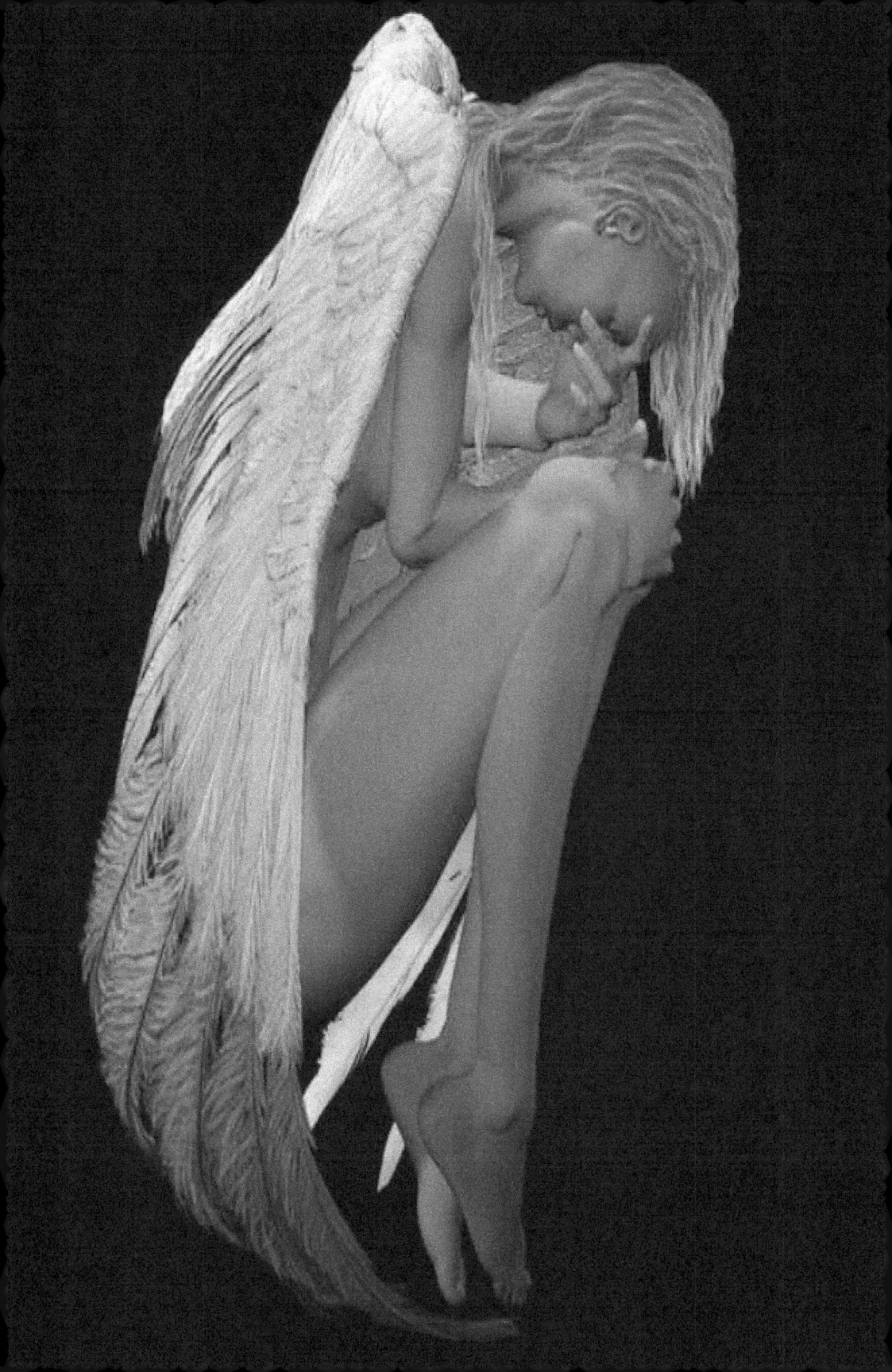

Dear God

A wind blew and put me in a state

No, not lost

Just in a state no word has yet found

A way to state

Just how this state feels

I lost myself in a forest of me

And every time I try to find myself

I lose a little more of me

I've drowned floating thoughts with a blaring TV

And fed silence deafening music

I've looked without to find what's within

I've been to hell to find heaven

Yet here I stand, alone beneath a weeping sky

Screaming at the one they say lives above the clouds.

Same

To feel everything so deeply

Is to live and die the same way

The deeper you love

The harder you crack

The darker the night

The brighter the stars

To feel everything as hopefully as I do

Is to fly and fall

The same

Way.

Writing on the Wall

We are all chasing something

Something is always chasing us

A dream, a life, the world

We are all missing something

All of us

Something's always missing us

Some of us

There is a god-shaped hole

In the center of me

There is a storm inside me

That has never been written

Never been calmed

Never been spoken

Never been seen

Never been heard

Only been felt

That storm is who I am.

I Painted This

Rain makes the flower grow,

Rain kills the flower that grows,

Was it him or I that wouldn't let me grow,

Is it the chicken or the egg that first knows,

Was it pride or shame that brought me low,

Was it I or love that first let go,

My eyes are glassed with tears that dare not rain,

My life is painted with all shades of pain,

What once I loved, I now disdain,

What once was me floats by no more again,

Tears tear down every wall of pain I once ignored,

Cold is a state that lets me be more,

With no hope, no reward,

Of love to keep me warm.

The road I paved was sorely flawed,

My heart is in heat with a song,

That pleads to find a home to belong,

This being has been hollow for far too long.

A lie after a lie became the song I swore,

The darkness became a cloth I wore,

To swim through life to heaven's shore,

This heart knows no law, it just knows war,

If I had been who I could be,

I would now have been who I should be,

The battle that rages in me,

Between who I was and who I am and who I will be,

Takes no cognizance of how or what or if I feel,

Or why I no more can see.

The fears in my head that keep me dead,

Are often by the monsters in my mind fed,

Fear and sorrow and confusion have only led

Me to curl alone beneath a broken bed.

Darkness stole me from the face of the sun,

The sun turned around and found another one,

The stars found me lying in the dark forlorn,

The sun loved me again when he saw that the stars would not abandon me.

Sorrow in her finite mercies floated these words to me,

And on the days I couldn't see
I painted souls,
And on the days I couldn't hear
I painted hearts,
And on the days I couldn't speak
I painted thoughts,
And on the days I couldn't feel
I painted desire,
And on the days I couldn't breathe
I painted air,
And on the days I couldn't live
I painted love,
And on the days I couldn't love
I died,
And on the day I died
I painted God.

Hometown

The things people do for love

The things love does to people

The people who love things

The things people love

The love of people's things

The people left when love leaves

The love left when people leave

The leaving of people who love

The loving of people who leave

The people who leave love

The love people leave

The leaving people love

The people who love to leave

The people who love the ones who leave

The people who leave the ones who love

The people who leave the ones they love

The people who love the lives they live

The people who live the lives they love

The people who love to live

The people who live to love

The lives people love to live

The lives people live to love

The love of people's lives

The love people forget to live

The lives people forget to love

The people who forget to live and love

The love to hatred turned

No one will hate you as much

As the people who once loved you.

Climate

If your head
Gets too cloudy
Don't look there
Look in your heart
I'm raining
There.

Court

We are all guilty of something, every one of us,

Hell is not for the guilty, nor heaven for the guiltless,

For we are all guilty of something, all of us,

The robe is not for you to wear,

Neither is the high end of a horse a seat for me,

For we all are guilty of something, you and me,

The hypocrite calls another hypocrite a hypocrite

They are all guilty of something, all of them... oh, of us,

The cradle holds innocence hostage,

We all hit the grave guilty,

The tree of knowledge corrupts all,

We eat of that fruit and we know... we know...

I know

I am guilty of something

When not me, then myself

And when we both are innocent... I

I am guilty of many things... all of me.

The Craving

We are but souls that crave from cradle to grave,

We are the ones that wave with and seldom against
the tides,

The day breaks, we seek the nightfall,

The stars twinkle, we want a full moon,

Loneliness departs from us and we miss the wisdom
in solitude,

When alone, we seek the voices of people to
accompany the voices in our heads,

The rain washes us, we seek the heat of the sun,

The sun burns us, we beg for a rain that weeps for
the sun,

Summer's too hot, winter's too cold,

Spring's too happy, autumn's depressing,

We crave for solitude, then a multitude,

We want ingenuity, without the insanity,

We rummage through history to create a new story
that repeats history,

We brave high altitudes, ignoring bad attitudes,

We take a fall, we become a wall,

We want it all, all we want is all,

A beginning with no end... but when it aches,

An end with no beginning,

We crave for friendship, laughter, water, air,

We crave for solitude without the loneliness,

We crave for company without the misery,

We crave for joy without the grief,

We crave for peace without a war,

We crave for love, for love, for love, more love,

We crave for life, and without the death we want the life after death.

Grownup

First you are born into the world

Then you ask why

That will be your first mistake

Every answer will question that question

When the hourglass spins fourteen times

You find a flame raging in you

You want to take a bite out of the whole world

You have a dream to do everything, to be everything

You join the rollercoaster that hitches everyone a
ride to the sky

You hitch a ride to greatness

Though no one you know has seen him

And everyone you know has missed him

You just know it's you - you'll be the one to kiss him

So the hourglass turns and the sands rise and fall

You have your dreams in your heart

And a pair of polished talents in both hands

So you dance and you sing and you write and you
act

You speak and you teach and you listen and you learn

You draw and you paint and you sculpt and you play

You are as you were and will be as you are

So you take a map and draw a straight line

From point you to where greatness is

You draw your lines and spread out knives outside the lines

You have a spade and you named it Spade

Your favourite colours are black and white

And your only friends are saints in white

You are wild at heart, born to see the world, born to be the world

On this side of the glass, all you have are answers

Answers to questions you never knew to ask

But in one last turn, you now live on the other side of the hourglass

On this side of the glass, all you have are questions

And jaded answers to innocent questions

You begin to learn that life is not a straight line

Your flame is now a flicker

Your dreams are now a distant memory of quiet
failures

On lonely nights, you dare to dream again

But you fear the day will break your dreams again

Your straight lines have become hills and valleys

The lines you'll never cross have been smudged by
bleeding blood

Your pair of golden polished talents became a
stolen pair of polished pennies

You used to dance and radiate your lovely strides

He asked you to dance and stole your pride

And all your symphonies died in you

The flicker in time became the darkness

In that darkness defining moment when your
shadow

Was no more your shadow but your reflection

You saw in you what you had seen in every adult
you used to know

You gazed upon your horizon

All your friends were now sinners in black

You sold your shiny talents for shiny dimes

A penny owned, a pride kept

So you have your money down in your pocket

And your head held high in the society

And hide the child screaming inside of you

Muffled in silence, in the darkness of your adulthood

Oh, all the colours of you drowned in a grey sea

And all the noise in the world brings you shaded comfort

So you never have to feel the chilling silence

Of all that has died inside of you

Of all the you that has died in you

So on you sway to the music of a tone deaf world.

Just Another Love Story

I will tell you a story about love

Love is a song you heard in the arms of your mother

That you spend your whole life longing to hear in the arms of a lover

Love is embracing the sun

Love is what the wind does to the tree

Love is what the tree does to its leaves

Love is what the rain does to the desert

Love is what heals the wound called time

Love is the times time gives you

Love is the aching distance between the moon and the sun

Love is a forgetting of old wounds

Love is a forgiving of flawed foes

Love is the hourglass that protects the sands of life

Love is the cut you got from mending broken people

Love is the breathlessness that makes you breathe

Love is the joy you feel watching him grow

Love is the seed you planted where a flower died

Love is the weed one person believed could become
a flower

Love is a word that is a glue

Love is a poem of innocence

Love is an arm that never lets go

Love is an arm that sometimes lets go

Love is what the stars do to an abandoned night

Love is a scarf upon your eyes

Love is a story of mankind written in Braille

Love is a poem your tongue writes on my skin

Love is an ear that listens

Love is the distance between two words

Love is a silence that says it all

Love is what company does to misery

Love is a friend that willingly loses his gavel

Love is a hand that lifts lead up

Love is a song the world has forgotten the lyrics to

Love is the song of all songs

Love is a song time cannot end

Reality is a nightmare we wake up from every time
we love

Love is a blind man that sees you clearly

Love is an eagle that laughs with hens

Love is fire, love is ice, and love is everything in
between

Love is a train, love is the terminal

Love is the journey, love is the destination

Love is what the winds do to the wings of a bird

Hurt is a story that leaves love bleeding

Love is a girl with eyes like a sea, and a boy who
lives to swim

Love is a boy with a soul like a desert, and a girl
whose eyes rain

Love is the soulprints you leave in my eyes

Love is what the lonely sun does for the earth

Love is what the wind does to your hair

Love is the rainbow after a storm

Love is a hand that holds yours during the storm

Love is a wind no one can hold

Love is a whisper everyone's heard

Love is a fire that leaves us burned

Love is the ashes that gives us life

Love is a truth that sets us free

Love is a dream you wake up to

Love is an idea that transcends reality

Love is the highest law

Love is an arm at your deathbed

Love is the darkness inside the tunnel

Love is the light at the end of the tunnel

Love is what picks us up after all is gone

Love is the twinkle in your eyes

Love is the dust in an abandoned house

Love is the blink between two sights

Love is what the light does to the darkness

Love is what thirst says to water

Love is what loneliness writes on your skin

Love is all the words you said in your lifetime

When all you really died to say was "I love you"

Love is a promise once upon a time makes to you
and keeps happily ever after

Everyone is a love story written in Braille

Love is the finger that dares to read it.

She

Some breathed against glass to know they were alive

Others bled by touching glass to know they were alive

She held her breath and bled words to stay alive

Some crawled in and out of beds looking for love

Some set every rule on fire, by the flame of love, in the name of love

On cold nights, her winter crawled into the summer of strange arms

Some wonder what the world means to them

Others wonder what they mean to the world

She lay in wonder of the dark world growing inside her

Some awaken by dawn

Others sleep at dusk

The day dusks in her, the night dawns in her

Some cradled the butterflies that became babies in their arms

Other cradled cold lovers in their warm arms

She cradled herself in her own arms

When the darkness falls, some count the stars

When the light rises, others praise the sun

She was her pride, she was her fall

Darkness is the place light goes to boast

Light is the place darkness goes to die

Some crafted songs from the desire of the crowd

Others wove songs for the beauty of their sound

Her songs were sewn from the fabric of a love that once was

Some hoped to amount to something

Others gave up and wanted nothing

She sat and watched everything

Fade into nothingness

Some ran from broken people for fear of getting cut

Other whole people tried to fix the broken people

She left their pieces on the earth and watched light flood through broken things

Some rested in peace on battlefields

Others in pieces fought wars for peace

She lay awake every night, the outside world in peace, and the world inside at war

Some drank their sorrows away

Others weathered the storms of sorrow

She drowned her sorrow in ink

Some looked up to the sky in search of God

Others looked down at their tears and asked for God

She looked inside and found no God

Some breathe against glass to know they are alive

Some breathe in then out to remain undead

Others bleed by touching glass to know they are alive

They bleed and heal and scar, and forever live in memory of the wound

She holds her breath and bleed words to stay alive

Her breath was the blood flowing in the vein of everyone she touched

Some loved to live

Others lived to love

She loved in war and died in pieces

She was his storm, she was his peace.

Horns & Halos

There is a fine line between evil and good,

A field that divides wrong from right,

A shadow that mimics the darkness and the light,

You'll find me there, walking on this grey sky,

I wore my halo at dawn, by dusk the horns were out,

Who am I in this war that tears my soul apart

The voices in my head of a divine friend and a subtle fiend,

I listen to both and incline to both,

My moral compass points me to that field,

Where I won't have to choose,

Where I just have to breathe,

Where I just have to be,

I am the image of an object that is lost,

I am neither good nor evil,

Dripping right and wrong,

Falling high and low,

Sleeping in darkness, waking up to light,

My conscience sits and waits,

For me to do either wrong or right,

Then grabs a stick to poke my heart,

When I do the wrong,

And makes a warm hand pat my back,

When I do right,

I've done wrong and I've done right,

I've known heaven and I've known hell,

But I've never known me.

Flight

When you put together the words:

A bird, a window, a broken wing

Then you put your mind to picture the words:

A bird, a window, a broken wing

Then I'd finally be seen

For all I have been.

Hope

Somewhere out there are a pair of eyes that are the window to my soul

I hope someday to climb that window and find my own

Somewhere out there is an arm the size of me

Nothing else fits it but the love inside I feel

Somewhere out there is a song in loop looking for words

My life is the lyrics to the your song

Somewhere out there is a poet penning my life

I'm just a poem in search of her poet

Somewhere out there is a rain in search of dry land

I am thirst, I am a desert

Somewhere out there is a desert dying for rain

I am a stream that wields a storm

Somewhere out there is a frame without a painting

I am a painter, I am the painting

Somewhere out there is a want in need of love

Somewhere out there is a blank page longing for words

My veins carry ink to my heart

Somewhere out there is a myth that is the truth

I believe in things no one can prove

Somewhere out there is a dream in search of a dreamer

I live to dream

Somewhere out there is a tongue made for healing

I am a wound with jaded scars

Somewhere out there is a you that I cannot see

And dreams have been the evidence of my hope

A silver lining will one day break on a dark sky

And it will have my name on it.

The Fingerprint

To trace where it all began

Find the hand that first touched my heart

To make my numbness feel again

Trace the love that first broke my whole heart

To know where my guilt began

Find the heart I touched and broke to pieces

To understand the destination of these tears

Trace the thoughts that talk to and cut my soul

To feel my breath against your skin

Stand in the rain and breathe in the fragrance after the rain

To heal my wounds without a scar

Touch me from my head to my thumped heart

To see the truth of all I am

Take a chair and stare my eyes to tears

To hear the sounds that stream my heart

Trap your lips and listen to my silence

To touch me when my life is dead

Search for immortality in these words I breathe

To trace where it all ends

Watch the rain fall upwards and my story begin.

Inner Me

Your best friend and your worst enemy

Hides in front of your mirror

You will stab yourself in the back

In front of you over and over again

Till you try to save yourself

Only to find yourself stabbing yourself

Your words will come back and bite you

Your thought's a sea that drowns you

Your skin is the enemy of your spirit

Your eyes are the downfall of your heart

Your actions prepare a funeral for your soul

Your past is a lover that never lets go

Your future is the flower hidden in the seed of the
past

Your mind is a prison you cannot leave behind

Your life will always be a show

A mask in the morning for all to see

A heavy heart at noon waiting for the night to sleep

A tear stained pillow carrying your fallen dreams

No one will ever let you down as you will yourself

No one will ever beat you up as you do yourself

All your victories will be defeated by small failures

All your strengths will kneel to a weakness that breaks the chain

You will conquer the world or die trying yet still be

Quite unable to conquer your own self

I have looked myself hard in the eye and found a truth to be, that

The only enemy that ever truly could defeat me

Has ever been the enemy inner me.

Some World

I know a home nature made of vine

We walked in and turned it into wine

We drank till our guts began to pour

Only then did our hearts walk out our mouths

I know a home weaved out of love

Only the blind live there, no faults swim there, no one sees them

As yet a child, I learned of a man who lived by the mountains

He loved a woman with all he was

And after he'd shown her all his heart

He died of a shaven head

I know of a land whose hands are free

With all its inhabitants locked in an open cage

A world where the mind holds the body hostage

A home where slavery is stitched to the skin of the soul of the mind

I know that life is war, that love is war

And all be fair in love and war

And that fairness is a word that has found no air in life at all

I know in wars some do die, and the rest do cry

What is a scar, but the mark of battles fought and a war won

I know that fear is as real as air to the fretful

And nothing is more real than fear to the brave

Who's scared, but a man who's taken one step back to look for courage

I know that the future is bleak to the man who weeps

Who is weary, but the one whose hopes

Got drowned at sea a million sunsets ago

I know a world where kisses turn frogs into kings

I know a home where all men live equally

I know a world that is free and free indeed

I see the sky playing with the sea

And the sun and moon finally finding a way to get along

I smell the fragrance the rain leaves behind

It's a smell of hope, a smell of life after all is dead

I know a world where love doesn't hurt this much

I know a world that holds no death parties between nations

I know a world where you don't have to die to rest in peace

I know a home where I laugh out loud with

All my billions of siblings around the world

I know this world, this home is all in my...

Head... my heart... my mind

I know above all I know, that the mind is the home

Where all great seeds begin to grow

Let's go home.

An Eye for an Eye

Things unseen... things unreal

Like the silent breaking of a heart

Pales in comparison to a growling stomach

And how your stitched arm aches more than

My forever throbbing open heart surgery, without anaesthesia

And how the world understands your pain but hard they try

Still cannot comprehend the wells called my eyes

Which all the days of my life hold heavy waters

That long to take a moonlit stroll

Along my wrinkled face,

The silence of the lambs. My pain. My cross.

The roaring of the lions. A quiet chaos. My implosion.

Immolate me with love, consume me with love.

Heal me with love. Love me with love.

What the eyes see the head understands

What the eyes see not...the heart comprehends

My life... it's been a journey through the darkest
tunnel

And none understood nay neither could
comprehend

How I could shine a light so bright in darkness

Nor how I could heal hearts with my broken heart

And how the blind could make the blind see

The eyes... oh, my eyes...

My eyes were blinded as all could see

But my heart though broken yet could feel

And comprehend

The eyes... the eyes

An eye... for... an eye

The head... for the heart

It's easier for the world to understand a bruised face

Than sympathize with a crushed spirit

It's easier to say there is no God

Than jump with eyes closed

No parachutes... no safety nets... just faith

Faith in something that cannot be seen

It's easier to hate and hurt others

Than to love and say "Here's my heart, destroy it"

Since I was young and now I'm getting... wiser?

I have never found true love

Born whole...

The more cracked the walls... the more the beauty

Oh, if only your eyes could see with all my heart.

Chess

A queen protects the heart of her king
I am the rib plucked out from your ribcage
Waiting for you to find me
And put me back where I belong
I am the protector of your heart
I am the lover of all things you
I am the moon that shines with light from your sun
I sit on the sky on a dark night
Waiting for your heat to ravage me
Waiting for your fire to consume me
I am the pawn that leads my king to victory
I am the lone neon light in your dark heart
I am the sands in your hourglass
I rummaged the world looking for love
Like one with a bomb inside her head
Looking for someone to explode in
I found no one, you didn't find me
Hence I imploded,
Checkmating my own world.

Grey Matter

Many a dark night

I lay bare on a naked floor

Staring the sky straight in the eye

Longing to see if it has a soul like mine

Hoping a voice will tell me I'll be fine

I hear nothing

I see nothing

Just a black canvas, just a blank page

On nights like those

Not even the stars

Not even the moon

Come out to play

Not even a sign that I'll be okay

I think of how odd I am

How I was drawn a circle

On a canvas painted with square people

Even in a black and white world

I'd still be grey

I long to be lost in a crowd, yet

I ache to be alone, just without the loneliness

On a night like this

My wrists are silent without a pulse

All I hear is the sound of heavy downpour

My skin is dry

The sky isn't crying

It takes a moment for me to realize

That it is raining in my soul

As black ink spills from my veins onto white paper

I'm reminded that

Even if I can't see the sun

It still exists at night.

...Day

I wanna die some days

I wanna breathe some days

I wanna dream someday

I wanna be someday

How do you live life by letting all go

How do you move on not knowing where to

Like grains of wheat that make a dough

My pieces need be bonded so

How do the seeds you sow

Hurt you like an arrow born from an arched bow

From high to low

Grown grass I mow

Weeds like thorns must leave

Snakes in the garden do deceive

A daughter of eve

Let my lonely heart grieve

Came, saw, not quite conquered

Still streams hear my heart ponder

Of many have I grown fonder

Yet all seem from me to wander

Leaving me here laying in wonder

Taking all I've seen, I have nothing left to squander

Happiness is hollow

Where it goes I follow

Though behind me pursues sorrow

Its pursuit makes me want tomorrow

Hope makes my heart mellow

And keeps me from six feet below

Greatness lies within my line of sight

What my heart lacks in light

My will makes up for in fight

When my hands fail in might

And my body quakes in fright

My spirit takes flight

I wanna cry one day

And let it all out that day

And fail no more no day

I wanna laugh one day

And fall in love that day

And cry no more no day

I wanna be great one day

And be who I am that day

And wear a mask no day
I wanna feel one day
And hurt no more that day
And hurt no one no day
I wanna live one day
And make my life count that day
And rest in peace someday.

You Rock!

When someone hurts you, your first instinct is to hurt them back. To make them feel a little bit more than what they made you feel. The same can be said of when you love someone. When my life hurts me, I've been known to hurt life back except the life that I'm bruising is mine... my one and only life. The same can be said of forgiveness. You withhold it from the ones who beg for it in hopes that they would hurt forever, for a pain they caused you once upon a flawed time. But my darling, it is you who begs forever. You beg every memory for life to take you to that moment when no one you loved needed to be forgiven by you. In time, you'll learn that everything begs for mercy... even your breaking heart. Then in that sublime moment, you'll let go of that rock which once was your floating rock, that's now nothing but... your drowning anchor.

Crayons

We colour the world,
Not with the darkness of our past,
But with the rainbow of our hope.

Ground Floor

Love is my sacred place. My home, my head, my heart, my storm, my shelter.

I gave you my heart, you gave me your heart, we made it our art.

You took back your heart, gave back my heart, I did the same and neither looked half the same for we had broken our art.

I wish that I could paint your heart as art upon a canvas that bleeds, so I could trace the moment you broke me into tiny pieces of you and made each piece love you forever.

The cold side of the pillow screams your warmth, a hundred 4a.ms miss our laughter, our weeping, our being. The crumpled sheets wonder why those two crazy kids no longer play underneath them.

On my heartstrings you played the most beautiful music my heart could bear, and when you tugged each string away, my heart lay beating on the floor.

Our bed is now like winter, only colder, so I sleep on the floor because it understands too well the weight of broken hearts. I spend each day on the floor writing letters to gravity, until the floor becomes a sea of memories that's thirsty for one more moment with you.

Gravity once wrote back saying: "Beneath the earth, the stars are legend. Above the stars, the sky is a floor. The floor you fall on, is the hope that helps you back up again."

I couldn't understand either half of that but in a way poetry has been my sky and my floor at the same time.

Love is my church. My heaven, my hell, my faith, my fear.

Yet my heart still hits the ground each time love makes a sound.

My Broken

You are my first
You are my last
You are my breath
And I will love you with my broken

You have my heart
You drum its beat
You take my hand
And I will dance with you, with my broken

You are my song
You are my scream
You are my silence
And I still love you with my broken

You are my home
You are my shelter
You are my storm
And I will hold on to you with my broken

You are my friend

You are my lover

You are my wound

And I will write you with my broken

You are my scar

You are my peace

You are my war

And I will fight for you with my broken

You are my wings

You are my winds

You are my sky

And I will fly to you with my broken

You are my saviour

You are my shield

You are my sword

And I will worship you with my broken

You are my pure

You are my passion

You are my pain

And I will touch you with my broken

You are my faithful

You are my pardon

You are my transgression

And I forgive you with my broken

You are my one

You are my only

You are my all

And I have loved you with my broken.

Close Your Eyes

You closed your eyes

Never to wake up once again

To this cold world

I gazed into your lifeless eyes

Dropped my bruised armour

And lay still next to you

I whispered life back into your bones

Wake up love and feel the sun!

Let it dry your weeping skin

Sing for joy

And sing for pain

Sing along to your heart's beat

Feel the love

And feel the burn

Feel the fire that sets you free

Write your woes

And paint your pain

Inject your passion in the earth's vein

Raise your hands and shout in praise

Raise your hands and scream for help

Let me know your angels' wings

Let me meet your demons too

I love you

The good, the bad

The ugly you hide in your closet

Your stars that shine and your loon moon

Wake up love and fight the war

Soon your dreams will give you peace

Close your eyes

Count to ten

Now is then

Winter's come and winter's gone

Spring is come, not yet gone

Open your eyes

And see the rose

That's growing inside you.

A Ballad of Me

A poet is a person who pours light into the world,

From the darkness of her own soul.

It's so dark in here and I...

Can see everything so clearly, except what's right in front of me,

Can count 2 10 everything that's wrong with me,

Can count precisely anything but my blessings,

Can state correctly anything but my feelings,

Can share freely everything but my curses,

Can walk away from castles yet carry the bricks inside my heart,

Can burn old bridges yet return to resuscitate the ashes,

Can be right yet oh so wrong.

Pain lives here and I...

Can't see the forest because of the trees,

Can't see heaven because of the firmament,

Can't see God because of the sun,

Can't leave hell because I am burned,

Can't love you half the way that I write you,

Can't see the sky 'cause it's covered with paper,

Can't feel the rain because I'm drowning in ink,

Can't leave you behind 'cause you've walked away,

Can't walk away because the road is smooth,

Can't not forgive you,

Can't ever forget you,

Can't say goodbye to your ghost,

Can't say goodbye because you keep saying hello,

Can't lose what was never mine,

Can't stop thinking about things that never happened,

Can't end this nostalgia for a place that was never home,

Can't see the carbon because of the diamond,

Can't see the beauty because of the face,

Can't see your eyes because of your soul,

Can't save my soul because of my body,

Can't find the words to write my own salvation,

Can't seem to find what was never lost,

Can't see the meaning because of the words,

Can't hear the thunder because of the clap,

Can't hear the music because of the sound.

It's so lonely in here and I...

Should stop by later right in front of me,

Should say I'm sorry to this broken girl,

Should say your moon shines brighter than the
stars,

Should say you are enough, just the way you are,

Should say I love you especially when I don't love
you,

Should fold this poem into her breast pocket.

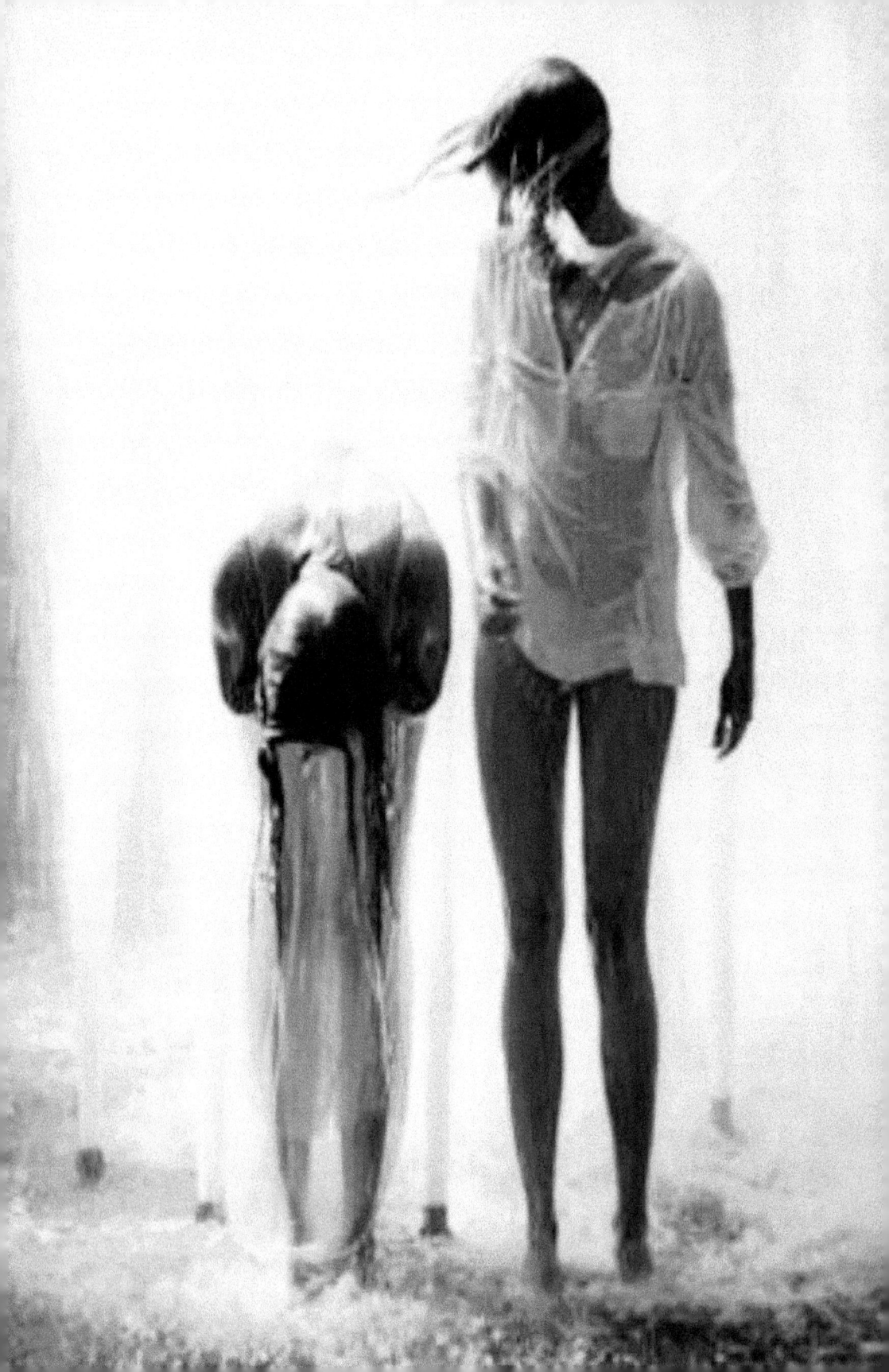

Bird

The things you let go,
Will someday teach you how to fly.

Go Away

You never leave
Your absence is ever present
In the roses you gave me
In the songs I shared with you
Tattooed on my soul with an invisible ink
In the wind which carries my head
To think of you again and again and then again
In the snow that numbs my hands
To reach for the feel of your touch again
In the sword that courses through my body
Like a roaring July rain
You remain here in the kindest part of my loneliest
hell
And your fragrance stains like a summer that
cannot be forgot
As the leaves hurriedly leave their trees for a home
on the floor
My dreams abandon me in search for another
reality
You are the music in my abyss
You never leave me
Your absence is ever present.

Questions of Science

These words are a map,

This map leads to nowhere,

The past holds no promise,

And the future is stained with question marks.

My life is a series of rooms,

With doors that have no hinges,

And when people come in,

They read my story for a while,

They pen love poems about my mind,

I watch the door closing as,

They jump out windows with no sill.

What makes you run away from me?

Is it my questions that mark no answers?

Am I a darkness that holds no star?

Am I an apology that's made no mistake?

Am I a defect in God's factory?

I know no answer and my poems pose no questions,

Only a poet's misery,

In this war for nowhere.

I just tell my story,

With my broken thoughts,

With pitch-black words,

On pitch-black paper.

Everything is made alright with a crooked smile,

Plastered across my breaking face,

For the ones who think that I am happiness.

There's a knock at the door,

My heart is bleeding question marks,

Yet he hears no answer.

A Tale of Ice

If you find me here
In this path forgot
Remember I was here
Know that I am lost

If you find me dead
Travelling this road I dread
Embrace me hard enough to shake me
Kiss me long enough to wake me

If you find these words
Hanging on your freshly painted walls
Read my heart that was once yours
Dry your eyes knowing it still is yours

If you find me no more
In flesh nor in memory
Know I knew not what to live for
Know I never want you to worry

I think of you less and less
Than I used to when you were mine to hold
Yet you haunt my heart more and more
Like it is yours to fold

My poetry is a storm asking peace to dance with her
To fill her heart with love and joy
And perhaps a drop or two of laughter
To wet this desert soil

Silence is the mother of my aching words
My silence is my self-defence
Silence envelopes my cold world
Scream at me one day from your cracking fence

If you find me there, with no sword, with no war
Left to fight no more
If you find me naked, devoid of mask
You'd find the answers to the questions you could
not ask

You've always been fire

I've always been ice

I wish that you could keep me warm even if I am on fire

I wish that I could keep you warm even if you were ice.

Talk

Let's draw a map from where we started to where won't end. You smiled at me from a distance, I smiled back. You kept looking at me, I couldn't stop staring at you. No planetary bodies existed except the ones rotating inside us. From hello to endless touches, my hands were carved for your body and yours for mine. I became a part of you, and you became my favourite part of me. I couldn't not feel you, I couldn't not need you.

Let's take the map and draw a straight line from here to where we thought we'd be. Everything is so different, oh everything is the same. You look at me from across the room, I stare blankly at your sculpted face. We wouldn't talk to each other, we'd just speak in silence. I won't admit I'm guilty and you can't forgive my innocence.

Let's stretch the line from 6pm to 11:59pm. The sheets are crumpled beneath our weeping bodies, we hold each other like we are all we have left in the world. We are all we have left in the world. I try to tell you that I'm sorry, you try to tell me that you'd forgotten... we had no words left but our silence. The clock struck midnight, the door closed behind you.

Let's draw a map from where we started to where won't end. The clock's still midnight every time I wake up. You can't forgive me and I can't forget you.

Let's close the map and have whole conversations with just one look again.

"I'm sorry and I miss you."

"You're forgiven and I love you.

Out of Breath

There is fever in my bones, an endless winter in my soul. My truth leaves burn marks on my chest. There is a storm in my heart, sometimes it's an unbearable quiet, sometimes it's just music — a record in loop inside me that breaks me over and over again. I've lost more than I care to remember, and I've been hurt more than I dare to forget. Loss is a lot like shedding your skin, except you feel every peel, and you die a little more each day.

It's unbelievably easy to not be yourself. You start out by living a lot of lives, by living a lot of lies. By numbing out every nerve with everything, and anything that makes you not feel what you feel... even if it's just for one night. But your heart never stops singing, and the song is beautiful even if no one hears it. The thing about not being yourself is that the you you fades slowly till no one sees you disappear.

There are nights when I've drowned in my own tears, and mornings where I've come up for air in words.

There are days when I wake up to the moon, and close my eyes at sunrise. I want to live again, I want to feel again.

So I try remember to live by forgetting all the places where I died.

There is a fever in my bones, an endless winter in my soul. I want to live my life dancing to the rhythm of my heart, even with broken bones, even in snow, and die completely out of breath.

A Slice of Heaven

You had heaven in your smile and hid hell in your eyes

Your smile was my sun and your eyes held full moons

I was too blinded by your rays to see your fire burning out

You were a harmony of sunrise and sadness

A sweet melody of hope drowning in despair

You were stained with rainbows and smelled like rain on a Christmas morning

You were a song that walked in uninvited through my ears

Jumped over my walls, and has never stopped singing in my heart

Your deep booming laugh still reverberates through the halls of my soul

You were an unforgettable symphony with no strings attached

You carried me to a crescendo that still hasn't fallen

I would have looked past your cover if I knew you were a book

I would have stained every page with teardrops laced with questions

I would have breathed you in and never again exhaled

But you had heaven in your smile and hid hell in your heart

And all my war prayed for was a little slice of heaven.

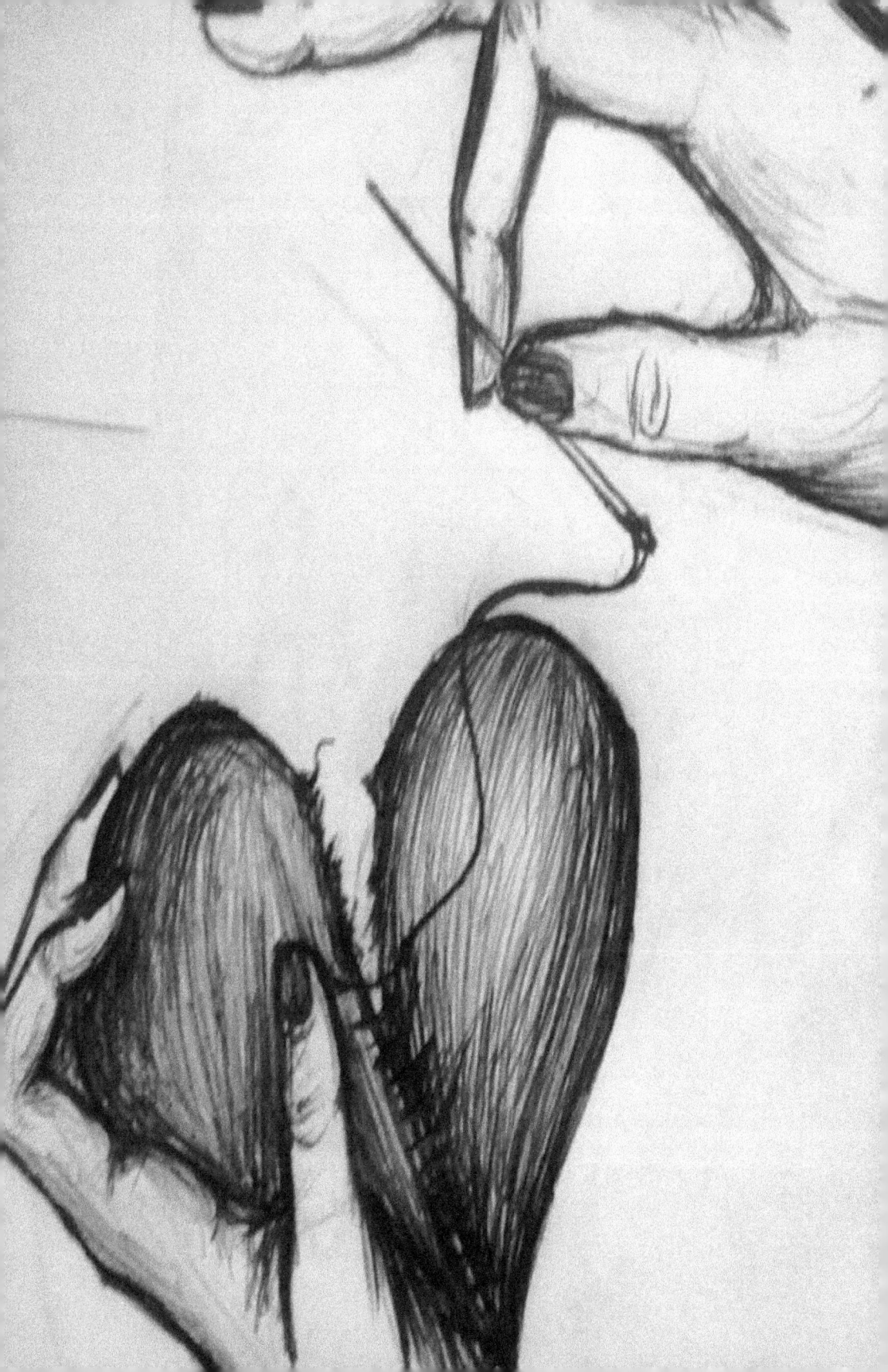

The Old Guitarist

A teardrop tells a story

Of the people you miss,

Of the things you've lost

Of the words you can't take back

And the things you won't give back

It's a story of your journey

Of the battles you've lost

Of the war you won

It's written in the stars in your eyes

It's written by the scars in your heart

And never ending battle wounds

It's a song of how you got lost

Of how you pray to find your way home

Of the moments you ache to remember

And the memories you can't forget

It holds a universe of pain

And galaxies of joy

It strikes a chord on your dusty heartstrings

It's the key to the vault inside you

And when the door opens

A flood crashes out

Washing away seconds of hurt

A teardrop is a remembrance

A memoriam for the things that died

And left graveyards in you

It's a triumph of the dreams that came true

When you weren't looking, when you were through

A teardrop is a photograph

Of what was

What might have been

What could have been

What cannot be

What could be

What is

What will be

Sometimes, in it you're smiling

Other times your eyes are closed

Yes, a teardrop is a poem

Of all you are.

Mindless Musing

I often wonder how many times we call the devil a liar

And if he sighs - "you are a liar too"

I've found the things we judge in people are the desires we hate in ourselves

The more different we are, the more the same we are

Altruism is so good a thing, it negates human nature

Every day is just a blank page time gives you

To rewrite your bad stories and make the good ones better

But accidents and coincidence cannot be ignored

For we all are preys of circumstance

We are prisoners of chance

And sometimes an invisible hand writes our story

And we just can't wait to know how it ends

I often wonder if the sun gets tired

If there are days he asks God for a day off

If the sun would rather go on dates with the moon

And take swims in waterfalls

It's easy to feel like God if you are the sun

Where all life will fade in your absence

I think of all the faces I've seen

And how they all mean nothing to me

Except the ones that knocked on my world

And the ones who let me climb their walls

I think of the ages as timed bombs

That explode inventions just in time for their age

The stone, the fire, the printing press, the cars, the industries...

Just like a flower, the world unfolds itself

You crawl, you walk, you run, and you fly

And when you have blossomed, you begin to fade

... Just like a flower

I walk into sunsets with people who walk away at sunrise

Yet at noon I look for another someone to abandon me

The abandonment hurts

But the joy in the walk makes it worth the pain

I think of silence, how quiet she is

And find that silence is a heartfelt written speech no one ever reads out loud

If you can hear the sound of a clock ticking, you are alone

If you have written poems from the silence between two ticks, you are lonely

I ponder on the desert how she looks just like me

The desert is a girl everyone remembers her name but forgets to love

The desert once wrote a poem to the sky; the sky wept all night

It is interesting how an idea transcends reality

Everything we see owes its existence to everything we cannot see

I watch everyone that walks by me

I notice how we all are trapped inside our own walls

Your walls are just a painting of the faces of everyone you trusted who hurt you

Art tries to recreate life

Every art, a piece of heart

A painting is a poem that has no words to say how it feels

We live, we feel, we love, we hurt

We craft everything that hurts us into art

Every tick of the clock tocks away a piece of us

So we desperately try to lock what's left of us in a white photograph

A photograph is a garden blooming a thousand words

Hope has been called a tragedy

That's fine, tragedy is when it begins to rain in your soul

Hope deferred can do that to you

Hope is a thread that cuts the moment you cross your fingers

That's how fragile hope is, that's how fragile life is

But without hope, you'd spend every waking moment wanting to die

And without hope all your days will be nights

Hope is that bird singing in your heart

It tells you "Come morning, the dark clouds will walk away"

I am a moth who loves a boy who is like the sun, his light is my life; his heat, my destruction

Love has never been the absence of pain

You smile because you have happiness

I write poetry to remember happiness

He sings to set sorrow free

She dances all her fears away

We weep to remember our humanity

The world is a beautiful place our hands can't help but break

Is love an arm with stones?

We reject those who are not like us

It's strange how sometimes all we love in a person

Are the parts of ourselves we see in them

I imagine a racehorse born in a time with no racetracks

How weird he must be to other 'normal' horses

Sometimes I feel like a faucet that no one has ever wanted water from

Sometimes I drip just to remind the world I'm still here

I remember the day I basked in the sun

I still have the scars from being shattered on the rocks the next day

I have found the more meaningless a thing seems

The more meaning it conceals

I have thought life to be meaningless

I have found love to be its meaning

I have spent these moments looking at him and her and you

And I applaud how hard you work, how hard you try to rise from the fall

At your final sunset you will find like I have found

That all that really counts is how hard you loved.

Run

I know how to run

Faster than pain

Faster than words

Faster than love

And everything that was born

To hurt me... deeply

But to

Feel nothing

Is to

Love no one.

Drowning

It was a tangerine-sky evening

When he caught the sun touching the sea

Ever so gently

Ever so fiercely

He ran into the water

To save the sun from drowning

Or save the sea from burning

He wasn't quite sure which

But he ran anyway

Sublimely into a memory

When she smiled at his sadness

And his eyes became the colour of her

In that solitary moment

Her sunlight dried his ocean

And no one could save him from drowning.

Addiction

Nine letters that swallow up infinite words...
infinite worlds. Nine letters written on your skin,
and on the pages of your bruised soul. Nine letters
I'd die washing away from your lovely bones. You
look so pale today. It's 2a.m and your ceiling is
stained with question marks. You shouldn't go
back, you can't move forward, and the ground won't
have you. Your wing is your chain. Your high is
your low. That which you can't live without is
killing you. That which you left behind is standing
in front of you with outstretched arms. You look to
me, our eyes are stained with the same colour. You
point to your scars, I point to a pillar made from
gold. You smile. I nod back. I go to answer the
door. You take his hand. I knock on your door. No
answer. It's 4a.m, your ceiling is now a vast black
sky with no question mark left.

Burned Bridges

My hands are tired of carrying everything you left behind,

My tears are tired of falling on waters you once walked on,

My eyes are tired of never really closing, of never really seeing,

My dreams are tired of waking to realities where they are not true,

My conscience is dead from carrying the guilt of my innocence,

My heart is weary from beating for the one who got away,

The tides have come and left me swimming where I was drowned,

The songs you sing, they break me, and make me

Search my palms for a map to take me,

To a time when the only thing I was truly tired of,

Was too much chocolate,

Was too much love.

Dark White

The candle inside you shines brighter than the sun

Holds more darkness than your shadow

Is more constant than change

The storm inside you is louder than silence

Roars like a lion

Cowers like a sheep

Shepherds your fears

To live your dreams

That thing inside you is a light

Sometimes a darkness

Always you.

Inventory

We've invented many things to take the pain away. And if they can't, we hope that they can distract us from it. Even the most innocent of us know exactly where to find it. Be it in music, loud earphones, drugs, alcohol, words, a person, blaring TV, inanimate phone screens, anything. Anything to make time rewind to times when everything was alright, or fast forward to a moment when everything is alright as they promised it would. Truth is, sometimes, no, everything is not going to be alright. Things are going to be messy, and monsters are going to crawl out from your soul onto your canvas or your paper, and sometimes, that too is okay. Sometimes that too is alright. So much of me has been washed away by time, and love, and heartbreak, and life. And that too is... alright. Except I want to smash something against a wall. Maybe crack the sky a little while I'm at it. Maybe with my screams, maybe with my silence... maybe with my tears. I'm still hurting, oh, so lost, and patiently waiting for that moment you promised time would heal me wholly, and make everything alright... if even for a moment.

Doubt

As black ink

Spills from my veins unto white paper

I'm reminded that

Even if I cannot see the sun

It still exists at night.

I Loved You Most

As I read you
I fell in love
With the holes
Between your words
And I loved you most
On the days
You could not love yourself.

Grace

Do you know what happens to me? I just started attending church again, you know, the broken home you call love. And each time a worship song comes on, memories leak through my eyes ceaselessly. I keep wondering why that is. I've been moved by music, always, but this felt different, like even though I thought I was now fine, there still was a gaping wound in the places I thought scars had grown. Each time a stranger calls me inspiring, or calls me successful, I give her a warm smile with the thousand suns that have set inside me. I'm not fine, I'm not okay, I'm not alright. But somehow, somewhere, sometime ago, God wrote that I should stay alive.

Dust

I said what my heart told me

And did what my hands could

I went where my map led me

And burned so many bridges behind

I held who my dreams made real

And promised you forever

My promise was eternal

But broke in time.

Parachute

Letting go feels like,

Falling off a cliff,

Slowly,

With your eyes closed,

Believing somehow,

You'll sprout wings...

Before you hit the ground.

I Should Know By Now

Before I sleep tonight

A fear will grip my heart

I've met this fear before

It gripped my heart last night

And a hundred nights before that

I'm afraid for my life

I don't know what I want

I'm uncertain what I have become

The days are growing dark

And I should know by now

But my heart palpitates confusion

And my eyes dart in every direction

In search of a nonexistent map

To show me where to go

To show me who I am

To lead me home

Before I sleep tonight

A fear will come for me

To turn my dreams to nightmares

To chase my faith away

But if you love me

Tie a rocket to me

So if I come crashing down

My hope will land upon the sky

Before I sleep tonight

I'll whisper a little prayer

Unsure of who'll be listening

Asking purpose to lay with me a while.

Him

I want to see the world through your heart,

To fall off the edge of the earth into infinities with you,

To fly, well aware of falling,

To fall, well aware of breaking,

Knowing you'll keep my pieces safe

In the chambers of your heart.

I want to feel all there is to be felt,

To laugh aloud as you watch me,

To moan when you touch me,

To mourn if you leave me.

I want to love you with all I am,

To kiss you with my last breath,

To hold you till your soul heals,

To chisel love poems into your broken bones.

I want to run wild with the wind,

And ruffle through your fallen leaves,

Till you laugh out loud as I watch you,

Remember what it feels like to be loved by me.

Creed

I believe in dreams

Even when they don't come true

I believe in hope

Even as I hit the ground

I believe in laughter

Even when no one hears it

I believe in God

Even if I never see Him

I believe in kindness

Even when I'm trodden

I believe in me

Even when I hate me

I believe in poetry

Even when I have no words

I believe in light

Even when I'm engulfed by darkness

I believe in trust

Even when it's broken

I believe in love

Even with a broken heart

I believe in these things

Even when it feels like

They don't believe in me.

Bliss

Forever is a promise
Not everyone can keep
The best loves can last a moment
Yet haunt you for a lifetime.

Self-Discovery

I keep losing
Myself
On the road to finding
Myself
In creating,
I have destroyed
Myself.

Desire

Show me what's not right for me and by loving it will I die. I'm not only wired to want what I do not need but I'm wired to want what I do not want. I'm drawn to red lights like moth to flame, and I'm pulled to things I'm told not to look at. I long for skies beyond my reach, and build my wings to surpass it. I want what's behind the heavens, to know that brilliant artist that hides his face. I'm like the ocean, bound by nothing, yet held back by an invisible hand. I'm like the sun, I rise and fall, win and lose, love and hate, hot and cold, fire and ice, here and disappear, lost and found... no middle ground. I want to know the universe inside me, but nothing is farther from my reach... nothing harder to defeat. I reach for the stars but my heart is a full moon, too cold to touch, too broken to crack. So I stand still touching things not right for me, loving it till I die. Breathless, not wanting what I want anymore.

Seasons

We love who we love because we love,

We are who we are because we are.

Sometimes people change, and remain the same,

Sometimes people break apart in two.

They love who they love because they chose,

They become who they are because they grow.

My Story

My story is a short one. I'm a girl. Maybe a woman. Well mostly human. Highly flawed. Low on oxygen. High on words. I write words, I sing songs, I paint my pain. The words are to touch somebody, anybody. The songs are to understand someone, anyone. Because it gets so cold out here, my lungs are filled with ice. So these words hold my hands and keep me warm one day at a time. So, I'm thankful for the eyes that read these words, and I'm grateful to the hearts that feel their poetry. Sometimes a touch sums all the words into silence. So read me until my words make you hold me... if even for a moment. Stay at least for one more day, and then another, just to feel how deeply my forever still loves you. I pray I leave rainbows behind after my words have rained. My story is a short one, well, not really. I'm a girl, maybe a woman. I create because that's the only way I know how to breathe.

Secret Crowds

There are people who know. Their skins are lacerated, and they lost their soul long ago. You wouldn't write poems about their eyes, and they'll always have too little to say and carry too much regret. These aliens are probably more human than you'll ever know. They feed on music and on the broken words of forgotten poets. They know the story of time, and can tell you just how many times time wanted to give up and be anything but sands in an extinct hourglass. If you can hear the sound of a clock ticking, you are alone. If you've written poems from the silence between two ticks, you are lonely. There are people who know, people who've seen it all, people who've felt it all. They've got more demons than their angels can save. They've lost more life than death could take. They lost their soul on the way to find home. Their eyes are music locked within a world without a sound.

Something Like Me

Sometimes you meet someone who is nothing like you,

Cut from different cloth - you're hemp, she's silk,

Born from different wars - she's a general, you're hiding,

She's flawed but she's magic,

She's the lyrics to your favourite song,

I met her where the road meets the sunset,

She carried me long enough to see another sunrise.

I met someone who loved something like me,

Till I became someone like me,

Her heart is a fire that cannot be put out,

She'll put off her sun just to touch your moon,

Someone who is quiet enough to listen to your storm,

And strong enough to look your demons in the eye,

Someone who sees you falling, but won't let you hit the ground,

Someone who doesn't try to fix your broken,

But asks your pieces to dinner.

Like a jigsaw puzzle torn in a thousand fragments,

I belonged to nowhere,

Till she showed me her heart was a castle large enough for two.

And we play in this castle, just us two,

And sing along to old songs we've long forgotten the words to,

As we did as children behind mom's car,

Long before we ever knew,

That sometimes you could meet someone,

Who is nothing like you,

Who means the world to you.

Numb Hurts

The easiest way to know that I was about to hit a rock bottom below rock bottom was how though life was gutting me, I felt nothing. This "bravado" came from an overexposure to pain. I developed a high tolerance for life wounds. Life brought knives to the table, all I had were words. There was a time when I desperately searched for this sixth sense called Numb, but having found it, I wish I hadn't. Pain comes in different variants - heartbreak, loss, abuse, lack, change, depression, separation, physical, psychological, abandonment, betrayal, regretting, remembering, forgetting... and once in every while, there is that one pain that has no name. You find yourself crying over nothing, or overtly sympathetic towards TV characters. I knew that I had arrived at the point beyond breaking point when nothing got to me anymore, when nothing moved me anymore. It was easy for people to mistake this for bravery but it was the absolute opposite, it was goodbye. So now my chest's heaving and my hands are trembling and my eyes are watering, and my lens is smudged, and my rear view mirror is crystal, and my mind is painting pictures of all the painful places where I died. Though this hurts a little more than hell, in this moment, in these emotions, in this place... I am most alive. And when this crescendo falls, I'll continue on my journey to find heaven.

The Bookshop

We are books.
And every book has a story,
And every book hopes to be seen,
And every book wants to be held,
And every book quivers for a touch,
And every book likes to be thought of,
And every book desires to be felt,
And every book aches to be opened,
And every book craves to be read,
And every book prays to be understood,
And no book wishes to be forgotten.

The Call

Looking through breath-stained windows,

I reach for your hand and catch air.

It takes a moment for me to realize that

I'm holding a memory.

It feels like I'm watching everything from space,

And in a minute, I'll hear my name and I'll wake.

But you don't say my name anymore,

No, not in that way no one else on earth

Knew to pronounce my name.

A way that told me you thought of me,

A way that said you loved me.

You are everywhere in my nowhere,

In every dream, in every song, screaming in my
silence.

The broken sky seems close enough to touch

So, I stand still in the rain and let it touch my tears,

I let the floor hold...

Everything life broke in me.

Elephant In The Room

Sometimes you try so hard to

Remain with the one you love

You fight so bad

And scream so loud

You let out flames from your lungs

Till the house is on fire

Yet neither of you

Wants to leave the building

Because this is the only home

You've ever had

It's the only home

You've ever needed

So you both stand still

As your hearts slow dance

In one final break

As your bodies fall to ashes

And for the first time

Since the last time

Your souls are happy

As your eyes shut

You are finally at rest

Sometimes you rise from those ashes

Sometimes you don't.

Lucky You

I see me clearly through your eyes

I'd trade in all the words to be silent in your arms

Joy feels like light, it's beautiful but it's created

Sorrow feels like darkness, it's ugly but it's creating

I've felt it all - the sun and the moon

The fire in my blood

The frost in my bones

I've seen it all - the lightning and the rainbow

The sparkle in your eyes

The last heartbeat of my hope

I've heard it all - the thunder and the silence

The breaking of my heart

The numbing of my soul

I've been it all - the star and the midnight

Yet all I want is to be with you

Through the daylights and endless nights

I want to sit with you in an abandoned house and still feel at home.

Destiny

I knew from the first time I met you,

That you'd either make or break me.

And you broke me,

Into every piece

That I was meant to be.

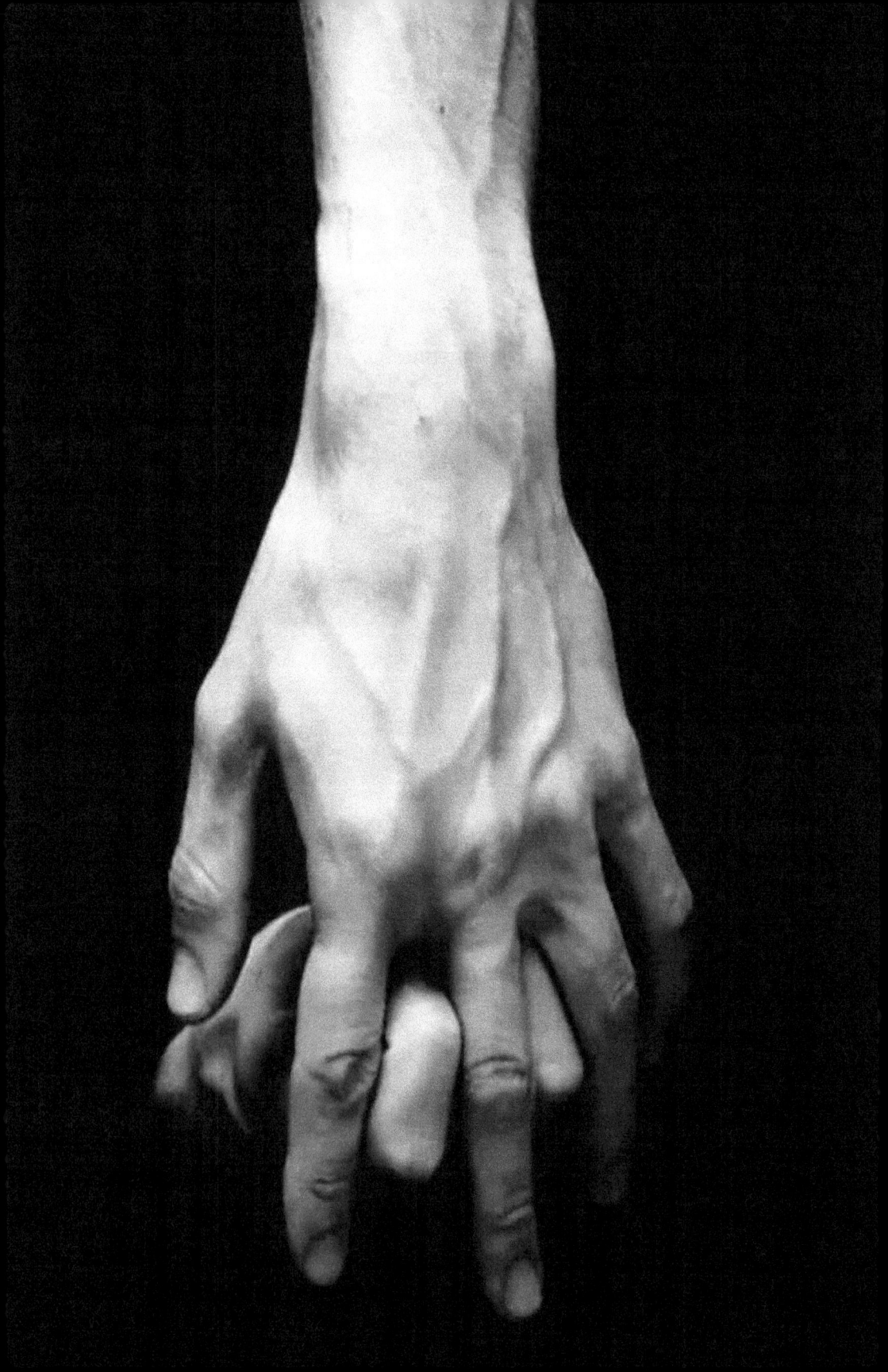

12a.m

I wake up in the morning and draw open the blinds. It's dark outside, it's always dark outside. I look inside me and find a match you left there for me to start fires with anyone but you. Every day had been a night since my birth, but when you found me, you sat as a star beside me and in the lightning of a moment, our laughter crashed through the clouds like thunder. But I was too dark for you and in time your shadow became your reflection. I had to let you grow and you had to let me know you had to let me go. There is no sound now, just clocks ticking with no second hand. My memories drown my thoughts in an ocean that's thirsty for you. I wake up in the morning and draw open the blinds. It's dark outside, it's always midnight without you. I spend each day in darkness writing about a light I once knew.

Let It Rain

I will not banish you from my broken heart
Or build graves in this place where you once lived
I will not wear black at the funeral of my loss
I will not look back at all I have lost
I will not write love poems in past tenses
As if love can never be mine, to give again
I will not let hurt define my reality
I'd rather let love remain my dream
I will not give up when the road is rough
I will not give in when I'm not tough
I will let myself fall to rise again
I will let myself cry to smile again
I will not let tears wash away my hopes
Nor fears extinguish my dreams
For every hundred bad days there comes a good one
One good one to surpass a hundred sorrows
One warm touch to fade my endless scars
It doesn't take much for an ebb to flow
I have seen things change that were always the same

I have seen dark clouds reveal a blinding sun

But if it must rain, then let it rain!

And if winter comes, then let it snow!

But in my heart burns a fire ignited by my soul

That does not flicker when I rise or fall

That will not grow dimmer in pain or joy

That will not go out through highs and lows

This fire is love

It burns eternal

It burns, eternal.

Good Morning

The quiet inside me
Is loudest at night
It says nothing
As everything cracks within me
Reminding me that I miss you
And the flowers that blossom when
You are near me
I long to pen poetry on your broken skin
And hang it as parchment across the sky
Watch as the stars begin to shatter
Exploding into a million daylights.

Immortality

We made it.

Through fire and ice,

Through desert and high water,

Through hope trickling down edges of cliffs,

Through screaming at an abyss that echoed our name,

We met the devil, we drank the deep blue sea,

We lived underwater till we learned to walk on water,

Silence gave us the truest words,

And pain coerced poets out of us,

Our eyes were windows to ever cloudy skies,

And oh did we rain till our pain was done.

As our spirits wander through mortal landscapes,

Let your hand in mine remind you that,

The hell in your soul will always find heaven in mine.

The River

You keep going to that bridge

I never thought I'd be jealous of a river

Life and death are one breath away

Love and loss are two waves away

Hope and despair are two halves of the same moon

You left your windows down again

For the rain to come rushing in

And carry you back to anywhere

With a river that makes you feel... at home

Holding your face in my hands

My heart melts in your universe

You're my center, you're my all

Nothing else can stop this fall

No one else can still this storm

You keep going back to that bridge

I never thought I'd be a river soon

But you're the ocean I run into

Time and time again

You're my fate and you're my end

So I leave my windows open now

For your tears to come rushing in

And for your fears to drown inside me

Everything you can't leave behind

And all the ghosts that haunt you

And all the water under your bridge

And all the stains that make you human

And all the things that I cannot see

That hurt you so much

That make you lost for words

I welcome them into my world

Walk in with your dirty shoes

Take the world off your shoulders

And lay it gently upon mine

I wrote you poems for the days

When you need a pair of unbroken wings

And sing you songs to pacify your dancing demons

I'll dance with you in your storm

I'll be your shelter

This is the only promise I can make

It is for you that I was made

It is for us that I won't break

But tonight

When I ran out of wood to keep the fire

Everything was still

Even silence was quiet

No rain rushed in

No wind rustled on our door

I ran down to your bridge

Like a poem in search of her poet

My knees crumbled as I held my face in my wet
hands

As I once had held yours in my trembling hands

And in one crescentic moment

I screamed and shattered silence

In one last breaking symphony

I went numb as my heart fell in pieces

Into a river that was you.

Unicorn

I'm often thought of as a unicorn

Like women who do not know what to do

With the flowers they've been given

Like people who know what life means

Yet don't know how to live

Like snow pouring inside

A burning summer

I'm sometimes called weird

Like aliens who don't know

That they are humans

Like sands that have no home but the sea

Like castles that have nowhere to stay but the air

I'm seldom named different

By people who understand what it feels like to be
me

To be a broken heaven

To be a fixed hell

To write of glorious stars

Yet be a cracking ground

To applaud love
With broken heartstrings
To pen a poem
When all you want to do
Is scream.

Aloneness

You are alone,

So alone,

You speak back to silence.

People call it loneliness,

You call it solitude,

Different words,

Meaning the same pain.

Home Alone

One day you will take a picture of yourself and you won't be in it. You will look for yourself and not find her. She would be buried underneath the rubble of your lies. And when you take a shovel to start digging, she would have run out of air. You have been everyone but yourself.

One day you will look for your smile and not find it. You would have used it all up in pretending to be happy, acting like you're okay, masking your disdain. You will trace your smile lines with your crooked hand and wonder what it feels like to smile from the heart. You have lived many lives but your own.

One day you will search for your heart and it'll be gone. You have given it out to everyone you thought was the one. Even when it was broken, you handed it out like party favours, hoping someone will hand you a piece of theirs in return. But no one ever did. And the ones you thought did never stayed. Now your soul roams the earth in an abandoned house. All you ever wanted to sit with anyone in an abandoned house and still feel at home.

One day you will look inside you and cry. Your matchbox is wet and the matchstick you once used to start wildfires inside you is short, alone, in a corner void of light. You will wet the pages of your story with the weeping of you. You who once was a volcanic eruption are now an avalanche. The goosebumps on your skin remind you that you can rewrite your story, even on broken bones. In the winter of her life she stared her night straight in the eye and finally saw the light.

One day you will look at yourself and smile from deep down inside you. Because that which was buried is now alive and that which was frozen is starting to spark.

Free

I want to be no more

In this place that hurts me

I want to feel no more

This love that haunts me

I want to see no more

This darkness that blinds me

I want to do no more

This thing that annihilate me

I want to run no more

From this truth that scar me

I want to run wild

I want to do good

I want see the light

I want to feel loved

I want to be

Free.

Vinyl

It's raining outside your soul

Some call it tears

I call it poetry

It's just a song in search of one word

It's just black and white

Staring at a grey world

Nothing fits

Nothing sticks on you

I don't fit

I'm not meant for you

Yet I was made for you

I was carved to love you

I'm written on your skin

I am the poetry of you

Your silence is a thunder

Your absence, a wound

That time cannot heal

Except with your presence

But you wouldn't want to be here

No one adores a thorn

Unless it's adorned with roses

Else it be but a weed

No one wants to see

Time never ticks anticlockwise

So why do I?

The past defines me

My pain writes me

I only wanted to tell you a story

That had no ending

No happiness never after

No sadness ever after

It's raining inside my soul

Some call it poetry

You call it tears

It's just a song I leave unsung

I'm just vinyl in a DVD world.

Beauty & The Beast

I've seen love do things to people - Turn beasts to beauties, calmed volcanoes into flames. No, not in fairytales but out here in the wild called Reality. I've seen people do things to love. Turn beauties into beasts, wield raindrops into floods. No, not in nightmares, but out there in the field called Dreams. I've watched love and people, I've seen people and I've watched love. I've touched heaven with the one, I've been hell without the other. I'm not sure what breaks who, much uncertain who breaks what. I've just observed that it's hardly ever love if it doesn't destroy you into more pieces than you are made of. I've only come to understand that you'd not recognize heaven, if you never seen hell.

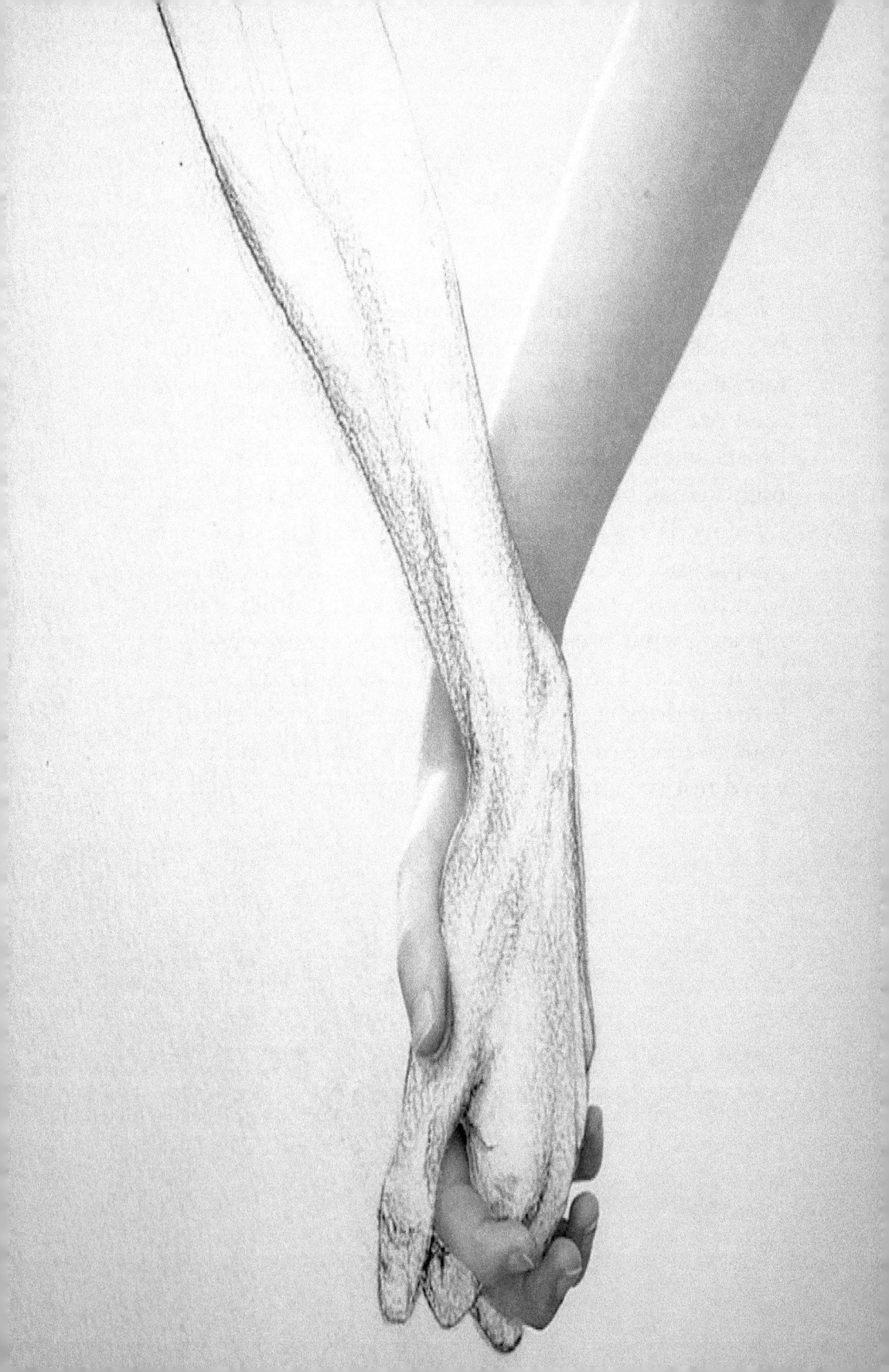

Mirror Mirror

"What do you see when you look in the mirror?"
That's got to be one of the most generic question
ever asked. More specific may be: "What don't you
see?" As long as you live, you may never actually
look yourself in the eye without a mirror or some
sort of reflective object in front of you. But you can
see yourself through the eyes of people and judge
yourself through their minds. And you would be
wrong. When you love yourself, no one can care for
you like you will. When you hate yourself, no one
can beat you up like you do. We all do things that
we are not proud of, we've all written stories we
don't want attached to our names. The trick to
living is in not defining you by your mistakes. The
trick to remaining alive is by not carving out
sculptures of your flaws. The little things make the
happiest lives - like a smile, like a memory, like
chocolate, like coffee, like a text message, like a hug,
like family, like a good friend. Conversely, the little
things also make the saddest lives - like a prayer
unanswered, like hope deferred, like loneliness, like
not belonging, like silence, like burnt bagel. The
trick is in finding one person (not necessarily "the
one") whose eyes see you in ways your mirror never
could. Who thinks you're still beautiful even when

you are broken on the floor. Who loves you most on the days you cannot love yourself.

What do you see when you stand in front of you? Your curves, your hair, your success, or your beauty? Your flaws, your loss, your pain, or your ugly?

Until you begin to see in your eyes, the people who define you as love, because they have felt a fraction of what's inside you, because you held them together when they were falling apart, because your eyes saw them in ways their mirrors never could, because you held them up even when it kept you down, because you loved them most on the days they could not love themselves. Then you haven't begun to live, no, you haven't begun to love. Not everyone gets the one, but everybody can be that one to somebody else. And if you are that one, staring one day into your rear view mirror, you will see a silent smile... you will feel a private kind of happiness.

The Bell

The room is quiet.

The paper is wet.

And the word "alone" chimes like a funeral bell.

The Language of Love

The language of love starts with deux
Two people who don't know what to do
The dialect of love begins with you
Speaking and understanding what is true
The ways of love are understood by few

I am me and you are you
You can't be me and I won't be you

The fire of love begins with this
A desire to know eternal bliss
A longing to feel an ethereal breeze
Carry away your troubled seas
Bring again your fallen leaves

I want you and I want peace
You've loved me in spite of me

The ways of love are pure and free
Free from hate, from rhythm and rhymes
Free from reason, from guile and pride
She forgives as she returns your bloodstained knife
from her back
She forgets what it is she wanted to hate in you

You are human

I'm one too

The hands of love are jagged and scarred
From holding on too tightly, from letting go too
quickly
From setting souls free, from carrying hope's dream
From falling on, from rising from
From caring for, from healing wounds

I am your you
You are my me

The laws of love are weightless with pardon

The robe of hate is stained with blood only love can
cleanse
The questions of life are answered in love
The story of love starts on a crowded street
The highway of love ends in a lonely country

You came alone
I go alone

The time for love is always forever
The timing of love can be now or never
The pain of love has carved accidental poets
The pang of love transcends time
Saying goodbye before you say hello, saying hello
after you've said goodbye

To be with you
To be for you

The language of love starts with deux
I'm fluent in you and the things you do
I'm fluent in you and the things you'll never say
The ah, be, see, dee of your soul
I'm free of you, I'm bound by you

I will live for you
I have died for you.

Family

The ones who love your dark,
Are the only light you'll ever need.

The Things That Hurt

The things that hurt the most are the things we love the most. With every bag of pleasure comes a chip of pain. Everything is interwoven. Life is woven with death, joy is woven by sorrow, droplets of sunlight after a flood of rain. You will feel everything - love, hate, passion, pain, laughter, tears, hope, despair, fear, courage, weakness, strength, and all there is that demands to be felt in this life.

The trick is in remembering that - nothing lasts forever, everything ends... even pain.

When the pain ceases and you can feel love again, and when the tears dry and you can see clearly again, the last thing you'd want to see is that your pain set fire to the ones you loved and that your tears washed away their ashes.

Always remember time, and how it heals everything it breaks.

What I Love

The things I love about you make no sense... not to love, not to hatred. The things I love about you are first your smile and then your heart. The way your eyes light up every time they catch me, like stars that have finally found a night sky to hang on. I like that thing you do with your hair when you think your world is coming to an end, I love how you believe me when I tell you it's just begun. I love your walls and how high they stand, I love that you trusted me enough to bring them down. I love how you tiptoe past cracked eggshells like they are pieces of you, you don't want to break. I love how you let me hold them like they were never broken in the first place. I love listening to the things you never say, I love when you tell me the things I never said. I love when you put one earphone in my ear and put the other in yours, and how you kiss me till I know that I'm your favorite song of all time. I love you wholly in my imperfect and in my broken way. I love you for reasons love cannot understand. I love you because my sun didn't have to set for your star to shine. I love you because night or day, we are each other's light.

The thing I love the most about you is your smile and how you share it with the world with your whole heart.

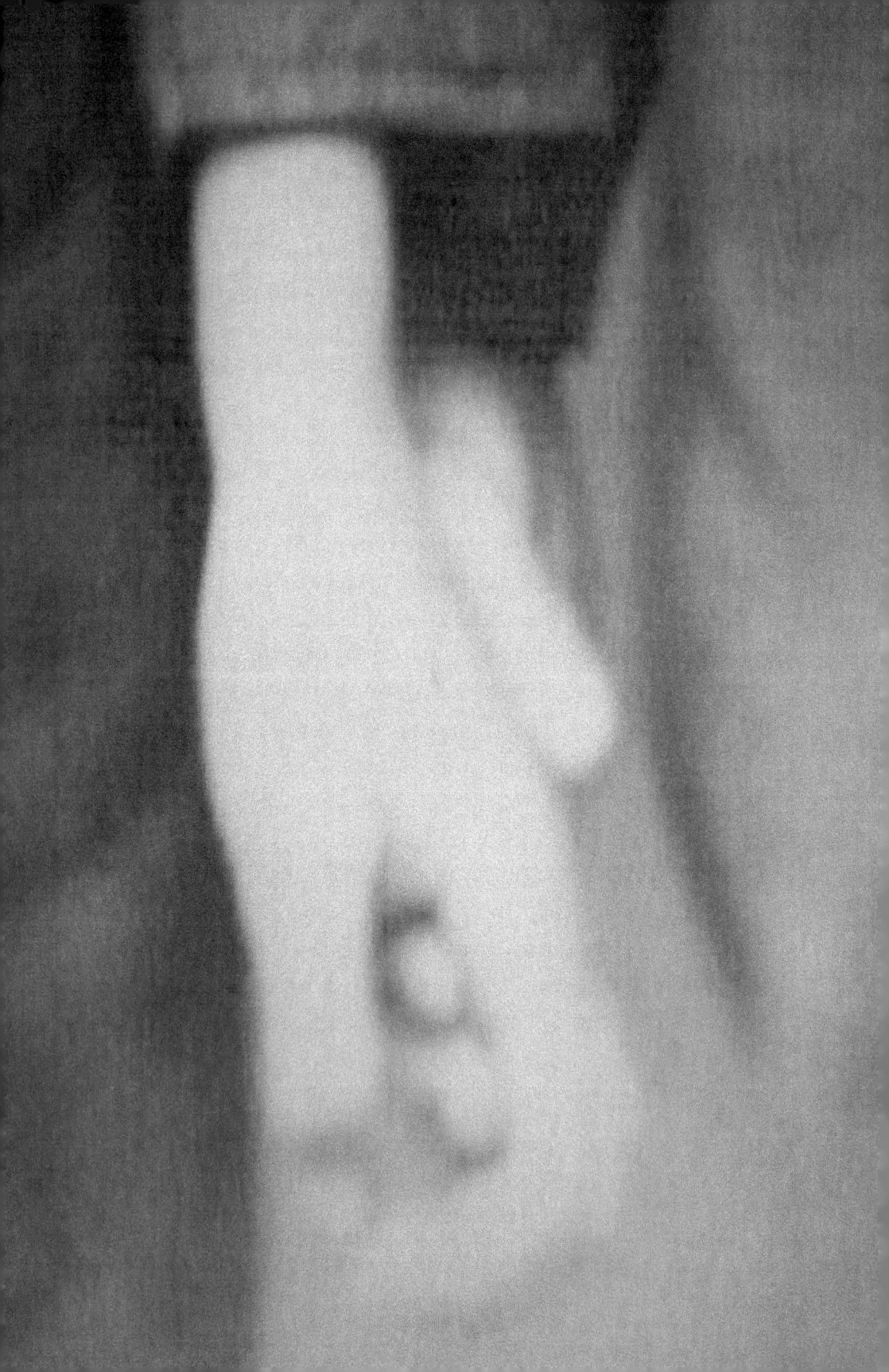

Your Dark

Thoughts of you fill my head,

As the moon digs a hole in my bed,

Even the starriest of nights,

Look pitch black without you by my side,

And every sad song seems to sing your name,

As I roll over to your side,

Teardrops warm the cold side of the pillow,

I miss you and your dark,

I miss you and the constellation in your eyes,

Every night they looked into mine.

Throw Away the Key

You are afraid to let anyone in,
But you still leave the door open,
Hoping someone good
Will shut the door behind him,
And throw away the keys.

Confession

To find that someone I can confess my sins to
without shame,

And still be loved shamelessly.

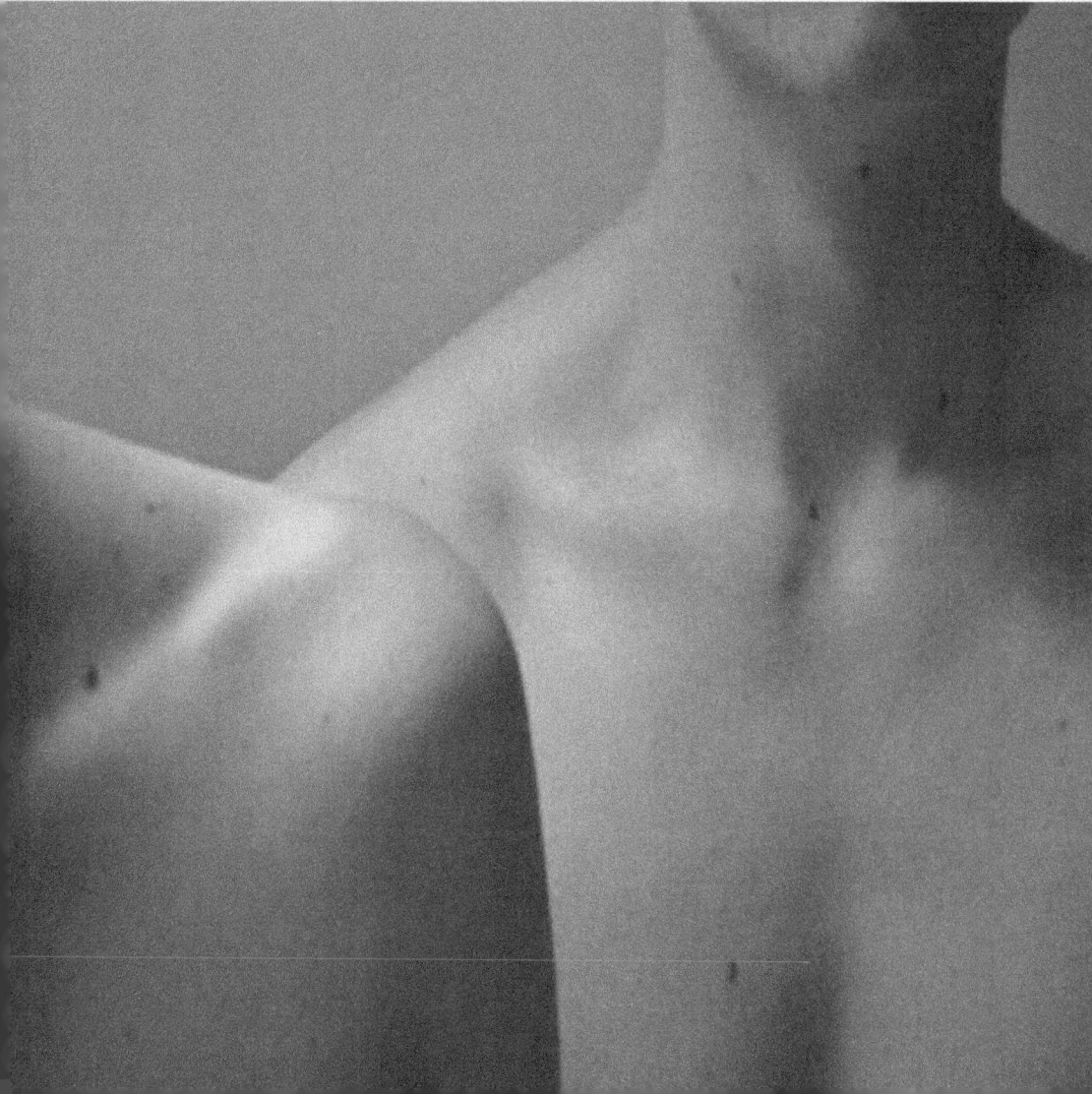

Heart

There would be no art,
If there were no passion,
If there were no pain.

As I Was

I don't know where to go from here,

So I crawl back inside me,

And

Turn the lights off.

Perfect Stranger

These words weigh heavier than my heart

Like light travels faster than the sound

In my head screaming for

My heart to be silent and

Listen to reason but

The only reason I'm fading away

Is because I do not know what or who I am

I'm happy then I'm sad

I'm lightning then I'm dark

I'm silent then I'm thunder

I'm a moon that wants to be the sun

I'm a climatic weather

I'm at once a storm and a shelter

A laughter and a tear

A clock and a wound

Your beauty and your beast

Rising from ashes to fall into fire

These masks are heavier than my face

My pretense highlighted at my reality

I have no one to be but who you think I am
I would be myself except I've never met her
My soul like thoughts can never be seen
Yet travels faster than the sound of words
That can only be written in languages
I do not understand
Explaining to strangers
Who I am.

Gold Digger

In all the places you find hurt,

Dig deep enough,

You'd find love.

I and Love and You

I write these words to touch you, my love, in places
my hands can only dream of. They hold you and
they tell you that I love you even when I cannot love
you. They want you, they need you, they read you,
they write you, they cut you to heal you because
they still love you. Even though time has written us
out of each other's stories, these words are the
happy ending we dared to dream of... once upon a
time. I'm sitting here stitching A to Z to fill a hole
love abandoned to silence. There is a wreckage
here, my love, that began when time let space make
me collide into you. The most beautiful words I
ever said was "I love you". The broken words I'm
still writing is that "I love you".

Love Letters

The moon fell in love with the night inside me

Sometimes all that the moon hides

Is just a broken sunset

Aloneness gave me words

To write letters

To the midnight

Inside me

Asking it to let me be

The sun or the moon

I'm stuck between the reality of remembering

And a dream of forgetting

So I keep writing poems

With open veins

And broken pens

In hopes that azaleas will one day blossom

In even the darkest parts of me

All the while knowing that

Words could never fill an abyss.

...eyes she saw...

...Pupils dilating.

...care about a' the risk?" he...

...uld care. Don't care when...

...curious warning pleading in...

...hing to lose,' she said fretfu...

...think I'd be glad to lose it. I...

...iefly. 'I am. I'm afraid. I'm a...

...she asked.

...backward jerk of his head...

...dy! The lot of 'em.'

...and suddenly kissed her...

Don't Let Life

If you let life, the first thing it would take away from you is your belief in love. That "doesn't exist" kind of love, you believed existed as a child. That pure and fierce love built to outlast lifetimes. That "however you are, you remain my person" type of love. Now, that kind of love sits in a shelf with God and dinosaurs and unicorns and such things high and old and imaginary. You start to accept whatever comes your way and settle for things that don't deserve you. And you begin to settle for anything that would hold you close if even for a night. Sometimes it's alcohol, sometimes it's drugs, sometimes it's a screen, sometimes it's a person.

If you allow life, the next thing it'll take away is your dream. What's the point of dreaming when none comes true?

You throw hope off a cliff and begin to be "real" about something designed for dreamers. Dreamers don't have the kindest realities - ask Joseph, ask Luther, ask Michael, ask David, ask me, ask anyone who's ever had a dream.

If you have a dream, guard it with your heart, even when it's been broken and beaten and bruised and shattered into fragments you can't even find. Guard it. With all your heart.

And the dream to love and be loved fiercely isn't one you should let go so easily.

Nothing about love is "real" or lives near the vicinity of logic. You don't forgive without an apology, you don't let go of something you love, you don't hold on to someone who hates you, you don't lift up someone when you're down, you don't fight a friend to save him, you don't teach someone how to fly when your wings are broken. Love defies reason, and that's the reason it is love.

Look around you. Most people are jaded, as if looking in a mirror at someone who they cannot be. As if trying to remember who it is they wanted to be. Remember your dream and fight for it again.

Love can grow in places where your seeds died, love can be a bird that alights upon your hand, love can be a river that flows from you, love can be a flower that survived winter. In whatever metaphor love comes, let it be the verb of your life.

Spring

It doesn't take a miracle

For seasons to change

One warm embrace

Can thaw a lifetime of winters.

Who We Are

If you love what you do passionately enough,

It becomes who you are.

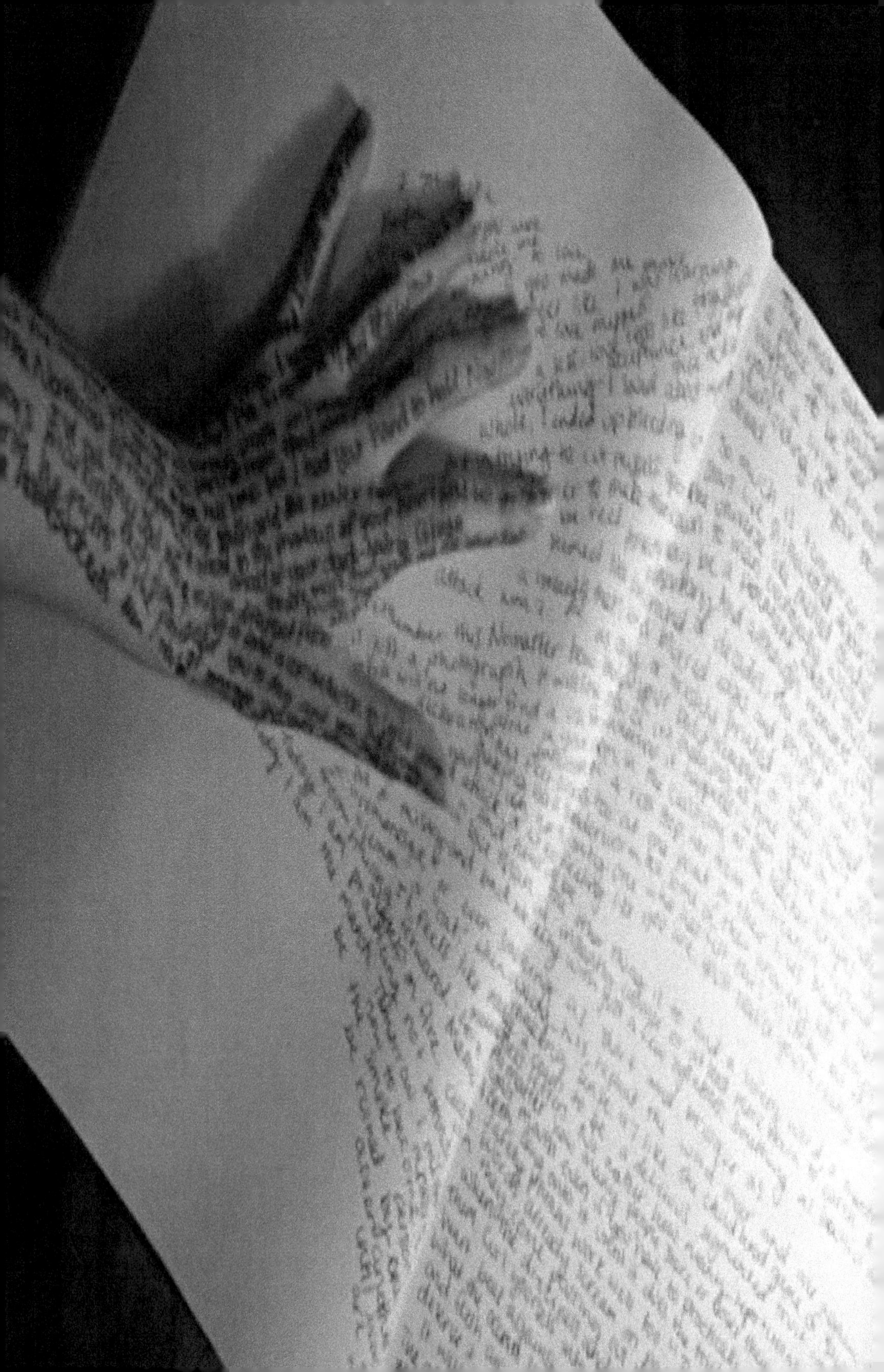

Lost In Translation

My first language is Silence.

Second, Thought.

Third, Speech.

My first law is Love.

Second, Love.

Third, Love.

Nobody

My feelings were drowning me

So I jumped into frozen water

I wanted to go numb

I wanted to know what it felt like

To be anyone...

But me.

Live

You laughed until you cried

You cried until you laughed

Your heart loved until it broke

Your heart hated until it learned, to love again

Soft breeze caressed your hair

Blue sea washed your feet

You swam shallow for fear of everything

You swam in the deep end for fear of nothing

A warm hand held mine

Another heart beat mine up until a single rhythm was formed

One day the hand left

Another held my hand again

And my heart got one more beating

Seeds came to you. You passed them on as blossoms.

Blossoms came to you. You passed them on as flowers.

Your smile did compete with the sun's shine

Your frown did compete with the moon's gloom

You sang and taught music a lesson or two

You wrote till your soul bled

You injected your passion in the earth's vein

Your knowledge spoke

Your wisdom listened

Your folly couldn't care less

You sinned and sought forgiveness

Got lost and sought redemption

Pushed against ropes

You pushed back

Betrayed. Forgave. Moved on.

Creativity and you were lovers

You and ingenuity, best friends

Failure knew you by name

Success found you later

The world knew you were here

The earth kissed you

I loved watching the sun set

Until today, when my sun did set

I have died a thousand deaths

Yet kept on breathing

But my lungs collapsed, on the night

When oxygen was taken away from yours, forever.

World Peace

There is still peace left in this world

And only those with beauty in their soul

Care enough to be it.

Karma

Though love's been all my heart could give,

Hurt's been all my heart could get.

.

Hope and Despair

The blanket of the sky warms the moon

On a cold night with memories of the sun

Slowly, the day breaks apart in dark hearts

And hope is born

Swiftly, the night falls on light hearts

And despair returns

It is not the one that is in the light that hopes for light

It is not the one that is happy that seeks laughter

It is not the one that lives that aches for life

It is not the one that understands that looks for meaning

It is not the fish in the sea that scratches the sky

With withered hands for a downpour of rain

It is hope that makes your eyes see through the mirror

It is despair that blinds and makes a glass opaque

Perhaps it is hope that makes me think:

I am the words in another's poem

I am the lyrics to someone's song

I am the rainbow in your grey sky

I am the lover of all things you

With hope, I clutch to life with one last breath

And when despair with one last breath clutches my soul

I remember the futility of all life is

And perhaps it is despair that helps me say:

I am the loving without a lover

I am a bottomless well filled with mistakes

I am but dust in the vast landscape of time

I am the roof the rain weeps against

I am the last piece to a puzzle that will never be found

I am the lover of every thing that annihilates me

I am the one who is lost and is found to be abandoned

I am the desert that swallows the rain

I am not ok... not okay

I will sit here till the world finds its full stop in me

O, despair is a monster that feeds on dreams

Despair sees the bad end of a good beginning

Hope sees the good end of a bad beginning

Despair seeks to die and not feel the pain of being alive

Hope seeks life in the throes of death

Despair thinks darkness is the only light

Hope knows that darkness is just a shadow of the light

Hope creates a thread for life to walk on

Despair seeing the end... cuts the rope.

Fate

The moon wouldn't be the moon,

If the sun could touch her.

Old Buildings

My house is made of ribs cracked open

Cavities filled with dust

Bones, the weight of lead

The walls are painted crimson

With blood sipping through countless cracks

The floorboards still cut my feet

With pieces of me I forgot had died

The halls are full of memories

The halls are full of memories

That fill me with an emptiness

No words can write or say

No one can see or touch

My heart is old with scars

And becomes young with wounds

Some days the scars become a wound again

Some nights the wound won't stop bleeding

The road to my house is

Covered in snowflakes and

Flooded with raindrops

There are no doors here

Just two closed windows

Only you can see through

Only you can open

My house is a soul dressed in snow

It's not much but it's all I have

And it feels like summer any winter you think of me

And it feels like home every time you drop by.

Shredder

I am a midnight torn

Between an ocean of hope

And a shore of despair

There are

Midnights inside me

That long to be a broken day

The things I needed to say

But never said

Shredded me into

Silent bleeding bits.

Forsaken

I've known heaven

And I've known hell

But I've never known me.

Iridescence

The first time I stood still under a dark sky was a quiet night. Nothing beautiful, no stars, no full moon, no half-broken moon... The sun had just set in me. Everything was silent except for the loud shattering of things inside me. My heart held a world of things that were constantly breaking, and this night, the few fragments left came crashing down all at once. I heard myself screaming up at the vast empty page that held none of God's poetry, I think I wanted the sky to crack and for God to place his hands on his ears as he turned away. After I had let my soul out, I walked home, except home wasn't home anymore, just another place I didn't belong to. As I inserted music into my ears to deafen the thunderstorms laughing inside me, I caught a flash of lightning slicing through the night sky. Suddenly, I felt water coursing through my clothes, touching my skin. I looked up at the sky and it looked just like me. The last time I screamed out to a dark sky was a lonely night, and since then these words have been my stars. The sun loved me again when it saw that the stars would not abandon me.

You Are Beautiful

The poems in your eyes are sad

Written by poets who touched you

Written by people who went for walks and never came back

Written by time and the wounds it cannot heal

Written with broken trusts and a relentless heart

Written by the dreams that came true and those that died to live another day

Written by promises and the fragments they leave behind

Written by the storms you hold back that peace may rain

Written by the tears you hide and the fears inside

The poems in your eyes are beautiful

In black and white

And in all the aching hues and shades in-between.

Me

All I need from myself,

Is to be forgiven by me.

Eternity

I've bled forever and won't die in time

My life became the distance A to where you'd B

I know what hell is, I've been in it

It's the absence of love, it's the absence of God

My thoughts often seek their freedom in words that bleed

Yet the silence whistles: "Find yourself within yourself"

So, I'm forever lost in the eternity of me.

Genesis

Every avalanche was once a lonely snowflake,

Every flood was once an aching raindrop.

Scarcast II

Everything ends. Nothing truly ends.

What has a beginning has an end.

Which is the beginning, the means, to another end.

The end of a thing. The beginning of another.

The end of a caterpillar. The beginning of the butterfly.

The death of a mortal. The life of an immortal.

The death of a seed. The birth of its fruit.

The end of a thought. The beginning of the deed.

The end of a word. The beginning of its work.

The end of time. The beginning of eternity.

The past behind. The future ahead. The past to meet again.

You can never truly run away from where you have been

The past carries all we are and the seed of what we become

When your story is burning out all your papers

Remember the middle of the fire where gold

And his brother, diamond are born
And strive to breathe long enough to see you
Thrive like only an outcast can.

"Write, write, write, write, write, write,
Write, write, write, write, write, write,
Write, write, write, write, write, write,
Write, write, write, write, write, write,
Write, write, write, write, write, write,
Write, write, write, write, write, write,
Till the pain stops."

-A Poet.

ABOUT THE AUTHOR

Jenim Dibie is a poet and writer. She is the author of the poetry collection, Scarcast. She loves music, photography and all forms of art. Her poetry swings between melancholy, longing and hope. She writes about love, loss, life, death, and everything in between. She writes regularly on Twitter: @scarville, and Instagram: poetetmisery.

CPSIA information can be obtained
at www.ICGtesting.com
Printed in the USA
LVHW03s1708100618
580220LV00003B/671/P